Foreword

When the opportunity arose to be associated with 'Where to Go
in Spain', we were particularly delighted. Harold Dennis-Jones
has produced a very readable book packed not only with
practical information about mainland Spain and The Balearic
Islands, but also with the sort of personal observations that add
that special dash of flavour.

As the leading holiday company operating in Spain, we
recognise the need for detailed information and guidance for
the would-be traveller. Here at last is a book, covering over
130 resorts, which answers all the questions, written in the
impartial and highly personal style of someone who knows and
loves this unique country.

Whether you are a committed traveller to Spain or a potential
first-timer, we are sure you will find this book invaluable in
helping you to plan your next holiday to Spain.

Thomson Holidays

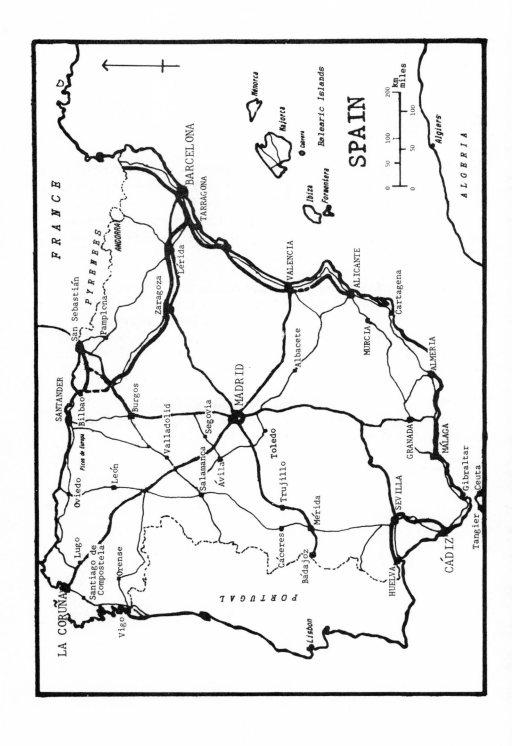

WHERE TO GO
IN
SPAIN

THOMSON HOLIDAYS

SETTLE PRESS (WIGMORE)
HIPPOCRENE BOOKS INC.

While every reasonable care has been taken by the
author and publisher in presenting the information in
this book, no responsibility can be taken by them or
by Thomson Holidays for any inaccuracies.
1988 Edition

Texts and maps © 1988 Harold Dennis-Jones
First published by Settle Press (Wigmore)
32 Savile Row
London W1X 1AG

ISBN (Hardback) 0 907070 42 6
       (Paperback) 0 907070 43 4

Published in United States by
Hippocrene Books Inc
171 Madison Avenue, New York
ISBN 0-87052-493-3

Printed by Villiers Publications Ltd
26a Shepherds Hill, London N6 5AH

Contents

1.	The Splendour of Spain	9
2.	Choosing Your Resort	11
3.	Choosing Your Holiday	17
4.	The Costa Brava and the Costa Dorada	22
5.	Majorca, Menorca, Ibiza and Formentera	41
6.	The Rest of Spain's Eastern Med Coast	70
7.	Spain's Southern Coast	80
8.	Hidden Spain	100
9.	Land, History and Culture	123
10.	Useful Information	134
11.	Language Guide	146

Maps

Spain	Frontispiece
Costa Brava and Costa Dorada	23
Majorca	42
Menorca, Ibiza and Formentera	60
The Rest of Spain's Eastern Coast	72
Spain's Southern Coast	82

Detailed Contents

**1 THE SPLENDOUR OF
  SPAIN** 9
**2 CHOOSING YOUR
  RESORT** 11
**3 CHOOSING YOUR
  HOLIDAY** 17
When to go 17
Package tour . . . ? 18
Or on your own . . . ? 19
Transport and other essentials 20

**4 THE COSTA BRAVA
  AND THE COSTA
  DORADA** 22

The Costa Brava resorts 24
Port Bou 24
Llansá 24
Puerto de la Selva 24
Cadaqués and Port Lligat 25
Rosas 25
Ampuriabrava 26
La Escala 26
Ampurias 26
Estartit 26
Bagur 27
Sa Riera 27
Aiguablava 27
Tamariú 28
Llafranch 28
Calella de Palafrugell 28
Palamós 29
Playa de Aro 29
S'Agaró 29
San Feliú de Guixols 29
Santa Cristina de Aro 30
Tossa de Mar 30
Lloret de Mar 31
Blanes 31

The Costa Dorada resorts 32
Malgrat 32
Santa Susana 33
Pineda 33
Calella de la Costa 33
Gavamar and Casteldefells 34
Sitges 34
Villaneuva y Geltrú 35
Salou 35
Cambrils 35
Tortosa 35

Excursions 35
Perpignan 36
Gerona 36

Figueras 36
Sierra del Montseny 36
Barcelona 37
Tarragona 39
Montserrat monastery 40
Poblet and San Cugat 40

**5 MAJORCA, MENORCA,
  IBIZA, AND
  FORMENTERA** 41

Majorca and its resorts 43
Large and lively 44
El Arenal (with C'an Pastilla, Las
Maravillas, Playa de Palma/
Playas de Mallorca) 44
Magalluf 45

*Not too large and not too
quiet* 45
Palma Nova 45
C'an Picafort 46
Puerto de Alcudia 46
Aucanada 47
Puerto Pollença 47
Cala Millor 47
Cala d'Or 48

Quiet and peaceful 48
Playa de Canyamels 48
Costa de los Pinos 48
Cala Bona 48
Sa Coma 49
S'Illot 49
Porto Cristo 49
Calas de Mallorca 49
Porto Colom 49
Cala Marsal 49
Cala Ferrera 49
Porto Petro 49
Cala Mondragó 49
Cala Santanyi 50
Colonia Sant Jordi 50
Cala Major 50
Sant Agusti 50
Illetas 50
Cala Viña 51
Santa Ponça 51
Fornells 51
Camp de Mar 51

Work and tourism mixed 51
Puerto de Andraitx 51
Cala Ratjada 51
Puerto de Soller 52

The west coast 52
Estalllencs 53
Banyalbufar 53
Deia 53
Sa Calobra 54
Pollença 55
Cala San Vicente 55
Hotel Formentor 55

Some inland spots 55
Inca and Manacor 56
Petrá 56
Cuevas del Drach 57
Valldemossa 57
(Cabrera island) 57
Randa and Alfabia 57

Palma de Mallorca 57

MENORCA 59

Menorca and its resorts 61
Cala'n Porter 61
Binisafua 61
Binibeca 61
Punta Prima 61
S'Algar 61
Biniancola 61
Cala Alcaufar 62
Shangri-La 62
Son Bou 62
San Jaime 62
Santo Tomás 62
Cala Galdana 62
Cala d'en Bosch 62
Tamarinda 63
Cala Blanca 63
Santandria 63
Ciudadela 63
Cala'n Forçat 63
Cala Blanes 63
Naveta d'es Tudons 63
Arenal d'en Castell 63
Cala Morell 64
Mahon 64
Villacarlos 64
San Luis 64
Mercadal 64

IBIZA 64

Ibiza's resorts 65
San Antonio Abad 65
Cala Grasió 66

Cala Tarida	66
Cala Vedella	66
Playa d'en Bossa	66
Les Figueretes	66
Cala Llonga	66
Santa Eulalia	66
S'Argamassa	67
Es Cana	67
Cala Leña	67
Portinatx	67
Port de Sant Miquel	67

Excursions on Ibiza 67
Ibiza town	67

FORMENTERA 68
Playa Mitjorn	68
Cala Sabina	68
Pujols	69
San Francisco Javier	69

THE ISLANDS' YEAR 69

6 THE REST OF SPAIN'S EASTERN MED COAST 70

Resorts of the Costa del Azahar 71
Peñíscola	71
Alcocéber	71
Oropesa de Mar	71
Benicasim	71
Castellón de la Plana	71
Sagunto	73
El Saler	73
Playa de las Palmeras	73
Cullera	73
Grao de Gandia	73
Playa de Oliva	73

Resorts of the Costa Blanca 73
Denia	73
Gata de Gorgos	74
Javea	74
Moraira	74
Calpe	74
Altea	74
Benidorm	75
Villajoyosa	75
San Juan (Alicante)	75
Playa Arenales del Sol	76
Santa Pola	76
Torrevieja	76
Campoamor	76

The rest of the coast 76
El Mar Menor	76
La Manga del Mar Menor	76
Cartagena	77
Puerto de Mazarón	77
Aguilas	77
Mojacar	77

Excursions from southern east coast resorts 77
Guadalest	78
Valencia	78

Alicante	78
Murcia	79
Elche	79
Alcoy	79

Some highlights of this coast's year 79

7 SPAIN'S SOUTHERN COAST 80

From Algeciras to Cabo de Gata 80
Algeciras	80
Sotogrande	81
Estepona	81
San Pedro de Alcántara	83
Marbella	83
Fuengirola	84
Los Boliches	84
Mijas	84
Benalmádena	85
Torremolinos	85
Torre de Mar	86
Nerja	86
La Herradura	86
Almuñecar	87
Salobreña	87
Motril	87
Adra	88
Roquetas de Mar	88
Agualdulce	88

Resorts of the Costa de la Luz 88
Tarifa	88
Vejer de la Frontera	89
Chiclana	89
El Puerto de Santa Maria	89
Sanlúcar de Barrameda	89
Chipiona	90
Rota	90
Palos de la Frontera	90

Excursions from the Costa del Sol and Costa de la Luz 90
Almeria	90
Guadix	91
Granada and the Alhambra	92
Sol y Nieve	93
Orgiva and Las Alpujarras	93
Málaga	94
Mijas	94
Ronda	94
Gibraltar	94
Cádiz	97
Jérez de la Frontera	97
Tetuan	98
Tangier	98

8 HIDDEN SPAIN 100

Andalucia 100
Arcos de la Frontera	100
Moron de la Frontera, etc	100
Sierra de los Guajares	101
Yegen	101
Córdoba	101

Medina Azahara	101
Sevilla	102
Jaén	103
Ubeda	103
Sierra de Cazorla	103
Sierra Morena	103

Madrid and Central Spain 103
Madrid	103
Aranjuez	104
Toledo	105
San Martín de Valdeiglesias	105
The Bulls of Guisando	105
Sierra de Gredos	106
Ávila	106
El Escorial	106
Valley of the Fallen	106
Navacerrada Pass	106
La Granja de Idelfonso	106
Segovia	106
Sigüenza, Alcalá de Henares	107
La Mancha	107
Mota de Cuervo, Campo de Critana, Consuegra	107

West and north of Madrid 107
Extremadura	108
Bádajoz	108
Mérida	108
Cáceres	108
Trujillo	108
Salamanca	108
Valladolid	109
León	109
Burgos	110

The northern hills and mountains 111
Cordillera Cantábrica	111
Picos de Europe	111
Panes	111
Potes	111
Cangas de Onis	112
Espinama	112
Fuente Dé	112
Covadonga	112
Pajares Pass	112

The northern coast 112
Santillana del Mar	113
Altamira	113
Santander Coast	113
Castro Urdiales	113
Laredo	114
Santoña	114
Noja	114
Comillas	114
S Vicente de la Barquera	114
Costa Verde	114
Llanes	114
Ribadesella	114
Lurca	114

Spain's far northwest 114
Galicia	114
La Coruña	115
Vigo	115
Pontevedra	115

Bayona	115	Canfranc International Stn	119	**9 LAND, HISTORY, AND**
La Toja	115	El Formigal	119	**CULTURE** **123**
Santiago de Compostela	115	Col de Portalet	119	The land 123
Lugo, Orense	116	Sallent de Gállego	120	People and history 124
Puertomarín, Monasterio de		Jaca	120	Literature and music 126
Samos, Piedrafita Pass	116	Berdún	120	The art of food and wine 127
Ponferrada	·116	Ordesa National Park	120	The visual arts 129
Astorgas	116	Torla	120	Customs and character 130
		Cirque de Gavarnie	120	Tourism today 132
The Basque Lands	**117**	Benasque	120	
Guernica	117	Viella	120	
Bilbao	117	Aigües Tortes National Pk	120	**10 USEFUL**
Basque Coast	117	Andorra	120	**INFORMATION** **134**
Lequeito, Ondárroa,		Puigcerda	121	Before you leave 134
Zumaya, Guetaria,		La Molina, Super Molina	121	After you arrive 136
Zarauz	117	Prades	121	Getting around by public
San Sebastián	117			transport 136
Irun	118	**Inland Catalonia**	**121**	Getting around with your
Fuenterrabía	118	Seo de Urgell	121	own conveyance 137
		Ripoll	121	Driving laws 137
The Pyrenees	**119**	Camprodón	121	Eating and drinking 140
Dancharinea Pass	119	Bañolas	121	Sports and entertainments 141
Puerto de Ibañeta		Zaragoza	121	Other points 142
(Roncesvalles Pass)	119	Lérida, Teruel, Albacete,		
Pamplona	119	Cuenca, Soria	122	**11 LANGUAGE GUIDE 146**
Candanchu	119			

1. The Splendour of Spain

Spain's a country of enormous variety. You can choose wonderful vast, sunny beaches of gleaming sand, peaceful rocky coves with secluded, hidden beaches, bustling large resorts, and quiet, sleepy seaside villages. You can opt for spots that offer a tremendous variety of coach or boat excursions, those where a hired car, scooter, moped, or even push-bike is very useful for exploring. And you can even find charmingly serene, tucked-away corners you'll never want to emerge from.

The islands of Majorca, Menorca, and Ibiza - the Balearics - on their own can provide four quite different types of holiday - five if you happen to be a birdwatcher. And the mainland coasts offer even greater variety, often with the added attraction of being able to visit one or other of Spain's great cities and some of her most spectacular scenery.

You can also avoid the sea completely and revel in vast inland regions of mountain and forest, or ancient towns like Córdoba, Seville, Toledo, Ávila, Salamanca and others, whose names are legendary and whose atmosphere can be magical. You can enjoy villages and small towns whose appearance has changed little since the seven centuries of Moorish occupation ended five hundred years ago.

There are settlements like this on the coast itself, too. From a distance they are indistinguishable (except by having churches in place of mosques) from the white towns and villages built by the invaders' Moorish relatives in Northern Morocco a thousand or more years ago.

In the northern Pyrenees, in southern Andalucia's Sierra Nevada, in the high mountains outside Madrid, and in the still little known Cordillera Cantábrica, Northern Spain's extraordinary mountain range, with the Alpine Picos de Europa at its centre, you will find ski resorts to suit every taste.

There's excellent sailing both on the coasts and on Spain's many inland lakes and reservoirs. Throw in colourful riding holidays in Andalucia. Add fine birdwatching in Majorca as well as the Pyrenees and in the world-famous Coto Doñana southern nature reserve, and wonderful wildlife in spots like the Sierra de Cazorla and the Picos de Europa. Top that up with exciting coach tours and excellent fly-drive holidays based (if you so wish) on the exciting State-run **paradores** that are often ancient palaces, convents and the like converted into very attractive and relatively inexpensive modern hotels, always furnished in local styles and serving

9

local dishes. That gives you an idea of Spain's almost infinite holiday possibilities.

Most holidaymakers however are bound for the beaches - millions of them every year. Some smart-Alec Brits sneer at the "Costas", mostly without having ever sampled them. But Spain's continuing popularity, not only with the British but also with Germans, French, Dutch, Irish, Scandinavians from every Nordic nation, and people from many other parts of the world prove they are providing what extremely large numbers of people want - as they've been doing now for over thirty years and were, in fact, doing in some places long before World War II. And they're doing it very well indeed.

The fascinating history of Spain's meteoric tourism growth since the early 1950s has never been told, even though it contains innumerable lessons for everyone connected with the travel industry. Even more important for modern travellers and holidaymakers, perhaps, no one has ever set out to provide a readable overall view of what is, after all, one of Europe's most varied and exciting countries. **Where To Go In Spain** aims to fill this void.

It starts with a tabulated assessment of the country's 130-odd Mediterranean resorts. This is followed by suggestions on how to choose and plan the holiday you want. Then come descriptions of the four Mediterranean coastal regions, beginning in the north with the Costa Brava (the Wild Coast) and

the Costa Dorada (Golden Coast), crossing to the Balearic Islands (Majorca, Menorca, Ibiza, and tiny Formentera), then returning southward to the Costa del Azahar (Orange Blossom Coast), the Costa Blanca (White Coast), the newly-named Costa Cálida (Warm Coast) and the Costa de Almeria, and finally reaching the famous Costa del Sol (Sun Coast) and the Costa de la Luz (Light Coast) beyond it, stretching from near Gibraltar to the Portuguese frontier. All are clearly marked on the frontispiece map.

After the Mediterranean coasts comes a tour of the rest of Spain, including the very different Atlantic coasts, highlighting places you might like to explore during your holiday or at some future date - or read about at home. Only the Canary Islands, far out in the Atlantic, and odd Spanish settlements on Morocco's Mediterranean coast and islands off it, all strictly parts of Spain, are omitted. They're too different from what the knowing call 'Peninsular Spain'.

There's also a chapter of practical information that may remove possible snags from your stay - what to expect in the way of buses and trains and how to use them should you want to, what you need to know if you hire a car or moped, how to use the local electricity supply, how to change money, which days will find offices, banks, and maybe shops closed for local as well as national holidays, what to do if you run into serious difficulties, and so on. The book ends with a brief very basic language guide.

2. Choosing Your Resort

The idea of this table is to help **you** to choose a resort - or at least to give you indications of resorts that might suit your wishes. The assessments are subjective and not based on quantitative measurements.

RESORTS, for instance, are classified 'small' (S) when they *feel* small. They are described as 'village or small town' (V) when that is the feeling given off by the old part of the settlement. 'Modern' (M) indicates that the tourist resort part of a development gives the impression of being modern. MV indicates a modern resort with an older village or small town attached, VM an older village or small town with adjoining modern development.

BEACHES are described as 'sandy' (S) when their base is pure sand; as 'mixed' (M) when their sand is mixed with gravel or small shells; as 'pebbly' (P) when the beach consists wholly or mainly of loose stones; and as 'rocky' (R) when you actually swim from rocks (some 'sandy' beaches may have rocks beside or in the middle of them but still be purely sandy).

Except when it refers to 'young children' (C), the **'SUITED TO'** column must not be taken as giving more than fairly rough assessments of resorts' possible appeal. Obviously, some 'older' folk (O) will prefer lively resorts. Some 'younger' visitors (Y) will opt for total peace and quiet.

This column should anyway be considered jointly with the **'ACCESS'** column, which aims to indicate not only how easy the resort is to reach but also the number and variety of excursions available from it (which tends also to indicate the place's general liveliness). A resort described as both 'remote' (R) and 'suited to both younger and older folk' (YO) should suggest that it's one whose total peacefulness appeals to people of all ages.

'Young children' (C) is different. It is strictly reserved for resorts where vehicles are kept well away from the beach, where the expanse of sand is spacious enough for unrestricted play, and where the beach slopes gently into the sea.

No attempt has been made to assess **nightlife**. In general, every resort will provide some sort of evening entertainment. The bigger ones naturally support discos and nightspots and excursions galore. The smaller ones don't. If evening entertainment's vital to your enjoyment, make sure your travel agent gets detailed information from the tour operator.

The table needs to be considered alongside the main text's descriptions.

Name of Resort	Resort		Beaches			Suited To	Access
Costa Brava/Costa Dorada							
Aiguablava	T	V	S	S	S	O	I
Ampuriabrava	L	M	L	S	O	F	M
Blanes	L	U	M	S	O	F	G
Cadaqués	S	V	S	R	S	O	M
Calella de la Costa	M	MV	L	S	O	F	G
Calella de Palafrugell	M	V	M	M	S	F	G
Cambrils	M	MV	L	S	O	F	G
La Escala	S	V	S	S	S	O	M
Estartit	M	V	S	S	S	YFC	G
Llafranch	M	V	M	M	S	F	G
Llansá	S	V	S	M	S	FO	M
Lloret de Mar	L	MV	L	S	O	YF	G
Malgrat	L	MV	L	S	O	YF	G
Palamós	L	UM	L	S	O	YF	G
Pineda	M	MV	L	M	O	FO	G
Playa de Aro	L	MU	L	S	O	F	G
Port Bou	S	V	S	S	S	YF	M
Puerto de la Selva	S	V	S	M	S	FO	M
Rosas	L	M	L	S	O	F	G
S'Agaró	M	M	M	S	S	FO	G
Salou	L	MV	L	S	O	YF	G
San Feliú de Guixols	M	U	M	M	S	FO	G

Name of Resort	Resort		Beaches			Suited To	Access
Santa Susana	M	MV	L	S	O	YF	G
Sa Riera	T	V	S	S	S	O	M
Sitges	L	MV	L	S	O	YF	G
Tamariú	M	MV	M	S	S	FO	G
Tossa de Mar	L	MV	L	M	S	FO	G
Villanueva y Geltrú	M	UM	L	S	O	YF	M

Majorca

Name of Resort	Resort		Beaches			Suited To	Access
El Arenal (with C'an Pastilla & Playa de Palma/ Las Maravillas)	L	M	L	S	O	Y	E
Aucanada (see Puerto de Alcudia)							
Banyalbufar	T	V	S	S	S	YO	I
Cala Bona	S	VM	S	S	O	YF	M
Cala Ferrera	T	M	S	S	S	YC	R
Cala Major	M	U	S	R/SS		O	E
Cala Marsal	T	M	S	S	S	FC	R
Cala Millor	L	M	L	S	O	F	G
Cala Mondragó	T	M	M	S	S	C	M
Cala d'Or	M	M	S	S	S	Y	R
Cala Ratjada	M	VM	S	S	S	Y	R
Cala Santanyi	T	M	S	S	S	C	I
Cala San Vicente	S	MV	S	S	S	F	R
Cala Viña	T	M	S	S	S	YF	E
Calas de Mallorca	M	M	S	S	S	FO	R
Camp de Mar	S	VM	S	S	S	O	M
C'an Pastilla – see El Arenal							
C'an Picafort	M	MV	L	S	O	FO	G
Colonia San Jordi	T	M	M	S	O	FC	R
Costa de Bendinat	M	U	S	M	S	O	E
Costa de los Pinos	S	M	S	S	S	F	R
Deia	S	V	T	S	S	Y	R
Estallench	S	V	T	S	S	YO	R
Fornells	T	MV	S	S	S	O	M
Hotel Formentor	–	–	S	S	O	O	I
Las Maravillas – see El Arenal							
Magalluf	L	M	L	S	O	YF	E
Paguera	M	UM	L	M	O	YF	G
Palma de Mallorca	L	U	–	–	–	O	E
Palma Nova	M	U	S	S/RS		O	E
Portals Nous	M	U	S	S	S	O	E
Playa de Canyamel	S	M	S	S	S	YF	R
Playa de Palma – see El Arenal							
Porto Colom	M	U	–	–	–	YO	M

Name of Resort	Resort		Beaches			Suited To	Access
Porto Cristo	M	V	S	S	S	YO	M
Porto Petro	S	U	–	–	–	YO	M
Puerto de Alcudia	M	VM	L	S	O	YFO	M
Puerto de Andraitx	M	VM	S	S	S	YF	M
Puerto Pollença	M	MV	L	S	O	F	M
Puerto de Soller	M	UM	L	S	S	YF	G
Sa Calobra	S	V	S	S	S	YO	I
Sa Coma	T	M	S	S	S	YF	R
Sant Agusti	M	U	S	S	S	O	E
Santa Ponça	M	VM	S	S	S	O	G
S'Illot	S	M	S	S	S	F	R

Menorca

Name of Resort	Resort		Beaches			Suited To	Access
Arenal d'en Castell	M	M	S	S	S	FC	M
Biniancola	S	M	–	–	–	O	M
Binibeca	S	M	T	S	S	FO	M
Binisafua	S	M	T	S	S	FO	M
Cala Aucafar	T	MV	T	S	S	F	M
Cala Blanca	S	MU	S	S	S	F	M
Cala Blanes	S	MU	S	S	S	F	M
Cala d'en Bosch	S	M	M	S	S	FC	M
Cala 'n Forçat	S	M	S	S	S	F	M
Cala Galdana	S	M	L	S	S	FC	M
Cala Morell	S	M	S	S	S	FO	M
Cala 'n Porter	S	M	S	S	S	FO	M
Mercadal	M	U	–	–	–	FO	M
Punta Prima	S	M	–	–	–	FO	M
S'Algar	S	M	–	–	–	FO	M
San Jaime	T	MV	L	S	O	FC	M
San Luis	M	U	–	–	–	O	M
Santandria	S	MU	S	S	O	FO	M
Santo Tomás	T	M	L	S	O	FC	M
Shangri-La	S	M	S	S	S	FO	M
Son Bou	T	M	L	S	O	FC	M
Son Parc	S	M	S	S	S	FO	M
Tamarinda	S	M	–	–	–	F	M
Villacarlos	L	U	–	–	–	O	M

Ibiza

Name of Resort	Resort		Beaches			Suited To	Access
Cala Grasió	S	M	S	S	S	YF	G
Cala Leña	T	M	S	S	S	Y	G
Cala Llonga	S	M	M	S	O	YF	G
Cala Tarida	S	M	S	S	S	YF	G

14

Name of Resort	Resort		Beaches			Suited To	Access
Cala Vedella	S	M	S	S	S	YF	G
Es Cana	S	M	S	S	O	YF	G
Les Figueretes	M	MU	M	P	O	YF	G
Playa d'en Bossa	M	M	L	S	O	YF	G
Port de Sant Miquel	S	M	S	S	S	YF	M
Portinatx	S	M	S	S	S	YFCO	M
San Antonio Abad	L	MV	S	S	S	YF	G
Santa Eulalia	M	MV	S	S	S	YF	G
S'Argamassa	S	M	S	S	S	YF	G

Formentera

Name of Resort	Resort		Beaches			Suited To	Access
Cala Sabina	S	M	M	S	O	FC	I
Playa Mitjorn	S	M	L	S	O	FC	I

Rest of Eastern Med Coast

Name of Resort	Resort		Beaches			Suited To	Access
Alicante (San Juan)	L	UM	L	S	O	F	G
Altea	M	MV	L	P	O	FO	M
Benicasim	M	MV	L	S	O	FO	M
Benidorm	L	M	L	S	O	YFO	G
Calpe	M	MV	L	S	O	YF	M
Denia	L	M	L	S	O	YF	G
Javea	M	MV	L	S	O	FO	G
La Manga	M	M	L	S	S/O	YFO	M
Mojacar	M	MV	M	S	O	FO	M
Oropesa	M	MV	M	S	O	FO	M
Peñíscola	M	VM	M	S	O	FO	M
Torrevieja	M	VM	M	S	S	FO	M

Southern Coast

Name of Resort	Resort		Beaches			Suited To	Access
Aguadulce	S	M	L	S	O	F	R
Algeciras	L	U	S	S	S	O	E
Almuñecar	M	U	M	S	O	YFO	M
Benalmádena	L	MV	L	S	O	YF	G
Estepona	L	MV	L	S	O	YF	G
Fuengirola	L	MV	L	S	O	YF	E
Málaga	L	U	–	–	–	O	E
Marbella	L	MV	L	S	O	YFO	E
Nerja	L	VM	S	S	S	YFO	M
Roquetas de Mar	S	M	L	S	O	F	R
Rota	M	MV	L	S	O	O	M
Salobreña	M	VM	S	S	S	YFO	R
Sanlúcar de Barrameda	M	U	M	S	S	O	M
Sotogrande	L	M	L	S	O	YF	E
Torremolinos	L	MV	L	S	O	YF	E

15

SOME PERSONAL RECOMMENDATIONS

For parents with children all at or near toddler age – **Cala Mondragó**
or **Cala Santanyi** (Majorca), **Cala d'en Bosch** or the **Cala Galdana-Santo
Tomaś-Son Bou** trio (Menorca).

For couples or solos wanting a lively time – **Torremolinos** (Costa del
Sol), **Benidorm** (Costa Blanca), and **Magalluf** and **El Arenal** (Majorca) are
obvious big-resort choices. **Cala d'Or** (Majorca) is much smaller, and cosier.
San Antonio Abad (Ibiza) is simply smaller, provided your hotel's near the
town centre.

For unpretentious family relaxation – Try **Malgrat** or **Santa Susana**
(Costa Dorada), **Tossa del Mar** (Costa Brava), **Ca'n Picafort** (Majorca), **Denia**
(Costa Blanca), **Fuengirola** (Costa del Sol), and almost anywhere on
Menorca. But note that these resorts all have different characters.

For colourful background and a good range of excursions (especially if
you hire a car) – **Blanes** or **Tamariú** (Costa Brava), **Algeciras** or **Estepona**
(Costa del Sol), and **Sanlúcar de Barrameda** (Costa de la Luz) if you're
specially interested in Andalucia.

For peace and sun when you're not so young – **Camp de Mar** (Majorca),
Mijas (Costa del Sol).

For watersports, golf, and other sports in a wholly modern setting – **La
Manga del Mar Menor** (Costa Cálida).

Really away from it all – **Estallencs**, **Deia**, **Sa Calobra**, **Cala San Vicente**,
and **Hotel Formentor**, all on Majorca's west coast.

But there are so many Spanish coast resorts which each have their special
character that anyone's special tastes can be perfectly matched. This list just
gives some indications.

3. Choosing Your Holiday

When to go

What time of year you go to Spain depends largely on the sort of holiday you opt for. If you want to roast on a Mediterranean beach in the summer sun, June to September are the obvious months. In fact, official temperature records show that everywhere except on the Costa Brava the average maximum rises above 70°F at least from May until October. On the Costa Blanca (see Chapter 6 for the precise definition of its limits), the Costa del Sol, and the Costa de la Luz the 70° average is reached as early as April. And on the Costa del Sol it continues until November. For a month outside these limits the average daily high tops 65°. In the coldest months, December and January, average maxima everywhere on Spain's Mediterranean coasts lie in the high fifties or low sixties.

Wind and rain can take the edge off temperatures. Strong winds blowing off cool mountains certainly limit the Costa Brava's effective summer season to June-mid-October. In the Balearic Islands, too, wind can be a problem in off-season months. But because it isn't essentially a cool wind - it's actually France's **mistral** roaring southward from Southern France's mountains - you can sunbathe almost year-round in well-sheltered spots.

Rain obviously falls on Spain's coasts - but surprisingly little. In fact, it's only along the northern coast, in the strip of land between the Atlantic and the Cordillera Cantábrica, and also in the provinces directly south of the Pyrenees that rain is at all common anywhere in Spain. Irrigation for crops is needed everywhere else. Much of the southern coast's rainfall occurs at the height of summer, when it feels positively warm and can be very refreshing.

What all this adds up to is that, barring sudden bursts of unseasonal weather, you can have a scorching-hot holiday anywhere on Spain's Mediterranean coasts from June until mid or late September, and - except on the Costa Brava - a pretty warm one almost all the rest of the year. If warmth is a major consideration December and January should perhaps be treated as not too reliable. If touring around from some coastal spot - or exploring one or other of the Balearic Islands - is your objective, the 'shoulder' months, March or April till late May and Late October and November, can be very pleasant.

Spain's inland regions and the northern coasts are totally different. Mild-temperature rain is possible all year round on Atlantic-facing coasts and in the northwestern region of Galicia, though they are also decidedly hot in summer. The country's many mountain ranges have the winter temperatures you expect at high altitudes. Excellent ski resorts in fact exist in the Pyrenees, in the northern Cordillera Cantábrica, in the Andalusian mountains south of Granada, and on the heights northwest of Madrid.

In most of the rest of the country, on the so-called *meseta* tableland, the Spaniards have what they themselves call 'nine months of winter and three of hell'. It's baking in summer and can be bitter in winter. The short spring and autumn can be pleasant, but their dates are never too certain. That doesn't mean however that fly-drive or coach holidays won't be thoroughly enjoyable in the winter months - just that you should go prepared to face cool and possibly decidedly cold weather when you're out of your vehicle. In summer remember that the evening heat normally cools considerably in mountain towns and villages - and a great deal of Spain lies in fact in mountain regions. Coaches however are usually air-conditioned. Spain really is an all-year country.

Package tour . . . ?

A package tour is obviously the easiest way of travelling. You choose a holiday from one of the brochures put out by numerous 'tour operators' - the travel world's wholesalers - and buy it, either direct from the tour operator or, more usually, over a travel agent's

retail counter. One payment covers all essentials from the moment you report at your UK airport until you return there.

Package tours take different forms. They may include accommodation and full board (three meals a day). Or accommodation and half board - you buy one of your main meals, usually at midday, outside the hotel in a restaurant of your choice. Or just picnic, of course. Yet another possibility is self-catering accommodation: you are provided with a properly-equipped apartment or villa and buy and cook your own meals.

Whichever of these package types you choose you can normally rely on all the on-the-spot help and advice you're likely to need from the tour operator's local representative. This can be very important if you're not accustomed to travelling. Make certain however that representatives will in fact be within easy and regular reach. If the information isn't *clearly* set out in the brochure, ask the travel agent to find out for you. And don't be satisfied with vague statements like: 'There's bound to be someone you can ask'. Reputable tour operators will give your questions detailed answers.

If you buy a coach tour you'll get your accommodation and either full or half board (three meals a day or breakfast and evening meal, leaving you to choose and buy your midday meal) on your journey round Spain. If you opt for 'fly-drive' you will have your flights to and from the country and the use of a car for the holiday's duration. Your accommodation each night will either be booked for you, or you will be left to find your own.

One thing that must be stressed is that everyone really ought to be absolutely clear before they start paying for a holiday what they are in fact buying. A lot of money changes hands, and to anyone who knows the ropes and stands for even a few minutes in a travel agent's shop, it often seems that customers just don't bother to ask the questions they ought. Reputable tour operators fall over backwards to fill their brochures with factual details - which is a good reason for buying a reputable firm's product. If a good choice of excursions, the availability of baby-sitters, hiring motor scooters, having windsurfing lessons, or anything else is important to you, ask your travel agent to get the information from the tour operator for you. And *please* don't be put off with vague answers.

What are the snags of a package tour? In hard fact, very few. Lots of people dislike the idea of travelling 'in a herd' (as they sometimes put it, usually because they've never tried it).

The truth is that you're no more tied to the people you travel with than if you'd booked independent tickets on the same plane. On arrival, the tour operator's reps may invite you to attend a sort of briefing session, maybe accompanied by a 'welcome drink', to tell you what they can do to help you and what the resort's and the hotel's general facilities are. But you aren't even obliged to attend, and even if you do you don't necessarily thereafter have much contact with your fellow-travellers. With a fly-drive package you're totally on your own.

The only real criticisms that can be levelled against packages are (a) that in hotels you don't get as wide a choice of food as you might if you're travelling on your own, and (b) hotel staffs (and almost everyone else who looks after you) tend to imagine they know in advance what you'll want to do. But this second little snag besets almost everyone who's an obvious foreign visitor. And, luckily, it's usually very easily overcome in Spain, where people don't try to force their wishes on you.

Or on your own . . . ?

You'll probably need a little experience before setting off without a package tour's backing. But it's not really difficult. Tourist Information Offices, open during normal shop hours (see Chapter 10), exist in all major towns and resorts, and will give you all the help you need. Most, including those at airports and the like, will help you book accommodation on arrival, including modest rooms in guesthouses and private homes.

Spain has a very complete accommodation range - from modest, clean rooms in private houses to luxury hotels, with every intermediate gradation - at very reasonable and carefully controlled prices. You naturally won't find inexpensive private-house accommodation in purely modern resorts, custom-built for package tours - places like that don't have private houses anyway. But you will in all the towns where visitors go. And also small hotels that often provide excellent value.

If you're not too sure of managing

by yourself, one well-known tour operator runs a special package programme of resort accommodation in small establishments of this sort. Apart from being thoroughly enjoyable it's a useful halfway house to completely independent travel.

If you're wholly on your own and plan to travel fairly continuously from place to place, it's naturally best to start looking for somewhere to stay each day pretty soon after the offices open in the afternoon - say, about 4 pm. This leaves time for evening sightseeing, but limits the day's travelling. The ideal solution is to move not more frequently than every other day.

In resorts which don't consist wholly of modern hotels, especially those where older town areas co-exist with resort districts (as in various parts of Majorca, for instance), it's also possible to arrange on-the-spot rental of apartments. Outside the height of summer (July and August) surprisingly cheap and good lets are possible. But unless you have a very clear idea of where you want to go arrange to stop a couple of nights in a hotel or guesthouse close to your arrival airport and choose your spot from there. Most airports have Tourist Information Offices that will help you find a place to stay at. A good deal of advance information that will help you plan the details of your stay is also available from the Spanish National Tourist Office in London. Consult them first.

Transport and other essentials

There's no difficulty about moving around once you're in Spain - unless you're determined to reach some very remote village where the buses go only at times that suit the local folk. Internal air services radiate mainly from Madrid but also link the Balearic Islands and certain main provincial cities with each other. Trains and long-distance coaches cover the entire country, though again cross-country journeys may not always be easy. Town buses provide all the services local people and most visitors need. And taxis are usually plentiful and inexpensive compared with most Western countries. Hitch-hiking isn't illegal, but isn't recommended either.

You'll obviously find that travelling about doesn't seem the same as at home. And a crowded foreign bus or train will seem much more crowded and uncomfortable than the rush-hour discomfort you're accustomed to on your regular commuter route. But isn't that part of the fun of travelling?

The easiest solution, of course, is to hire a car or maybe a scooter (they're available in quite a number of resorts). Car hire can often be arranged in advance through the tour operator you buy your holiday or flight from. With car hire you can enjoy the advantages both of a package and of independent exploration. Scooters can't usually be hired in advance.

As in other countries, you'll find a wide choice of restaurants. Unlike other countries however Spain's are all government-graded, with maximum prices limited by their grading. Further, they're all obliged to provide a reasonably-priced set meal called ***menú del día*** (today's choice), and to post prices clearly. What you won't find is the choice of cheap snackbars and quickfood establishments normal in Britain. You buy picnic food in markets and supermarkets instead, and patronise the most entertaining-looking bar you can find for coffee and other drinks. The only snag about eating restaurant meals outside the coast resorts that foreigners flock to is that Spaniards never start lunch before 1.30 pm, nor dinner before 9 pm. That can leave you feeling very hungry till your stomach adjusts to local habits.

As for sports and entertainments you'll find that lots of resorts offer a choice of tennis, horse-riding, windsurfing, water-skiing, and maybe sailing-dinghy hire, with instruction for those who wish it. If you're making your own travel arrangements you should ask the Spanish National Tourist Office for information about sports that interest you. With packages the tour operator should be able to provide all essential information. Golf is a bit different in that golfing holidays are mostly organised by specialist concerns, who include the cost of green fees, etc in the holiday price.

All these topics are dealt with in Chapter 10.

4.   The Costa Brava and the Costa Dorada

Spain's Costa Brava starts at the French frontier and runs as far as the River Tordera, the boundary of Gerona Province, just south of Blanes. The Costa Dorada (Golden Coast) stretches from Blanes to just beyond the delta at the River Ebro's mouth, fifty miles south of Tarragona. It lies in the Provinces of Barcelona and Tarragona.

These two sections of coast have very different characters. The Costa Brava really is as wild as its name suggests. It consists of a long series of rocky bays and cliffs broken by sandy beaches usually set between craggy headlands, many extremely picturesque. The little villages and fishing ports that most of them contain are as colourful as anything you could wish to see, and it's often a long way round by road from one little spot to its neighbour a couple of miles away.

At Blanes the character of the shoreline changes. Though cliffs still occur occasionally, the wild rocky coves and very rugged slopes give way to much flatter land climbing gently up to inland hills. Barcelona is barely forty miles off and the coastal settlements become increasingly industrialised. Beyond, cliffs begin again as you approach Sitges. Then the shore flattens once more as you near the port and industrial city of Tarragona, with

Salou some eight or nine miles beyond it and a string of very minor resorts stretched along level ground to the River Ebro's large delta and the Costa Dorada's and Tarragona Province's boundary some 25 miles further on.

It isn't only terrain that makes these two sections of coast different. The Costa Brava, lying wholly in the province of Gerona, is Catalan. The northern half of the Costa Dorada, in Barcelona Province, is also strongly Catalan. But the southern section, part of Tarragona Province's territory, becomes more Spanish. Differences are bigger than you think. The two languages are different - much more basically so than you'd imagine just from hearing different Spanish dialects spoken.

Catalan history, too, is different from that of much of Spain. Catalonia was once a separate kingdom with two capitals, one of them at Perpignan on the other side of the Pyrenees in France (you can still see the former royal palace there). When Columbus discovered the New World and gave Spaniards opportunities for amassing untold new wealth the Catalans for two centuries were forbidden to trade there - even though they were then the Western Mediterranean's leading carriers. The Catalans lost their independence completely in

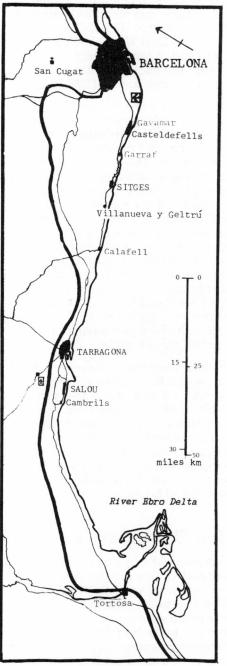

23

the eighteenth century, regained it in 1932, fought ferociously against Franco and the Nationalists in the 1936-39 Civil War, were again deprived of self-determination in 1938, and finally obtained a degree of local autonomy in 1977.

Today they have their own Provincial Assembly, meeting in Barcelona. But that hasn't prevented the continuing growth of Catalan nationalism. The only manifestations of what is in fact very strong feeling that you're likely to notice however is the fact that every town and village seems to have two names -as in Wales - and that in the cool of a summer evening groups of locals will gather in a town or village square and dance their stately **sardanas** to the music of a traditional **cobla** group. Nothing much actually happens. Yet the strength of the participants' feelings is often considerable.

Finally, the airports of Gerona in the north and Reus, close to Tarragona, handle the bulk of this area's charter flights. Scheduled services and a few charters operate into Barcelona. Airport-to-resort transfers are normally very speedy, unless you land at Gerona and travel to Sitges or Salou, which takes about two-and-a-half hours.

The Costa Brava's resorts

Just inside the Spanish frontier, separated from the modern motorway by some thirty miles of East Pyrenean mountains, and still the place where on most trains you have to move from French to Spanish rolling stock because of the gauge change, **Port Bou** today has a decided 'end of the road' atmosphere, despite a road frontier post on the low pass just above the village. If this is your first sight of the Costa Brava it's an excellent foretaste of what's in store.

Port Bou consists of a number of small bars and restaurants, one or two places where you can stay, a station and a small marshalling yard, a quite good beach, and very little else. There just isn't room for any more between the mountains and the sea. Even the north-bound railway vanishes abruptly into a tunnel. Nevertheless, the little town stages its own celebrations for the four days starting on the Feast of St James, 25 July.

It's a narrow, winding, picturesque road that takes you ten miles south over the cliffs and through a few tiny hamlets to **Llansá**, the first of the Costa Brava's older resorts. The little town is attractively set in its sheltered cove, and in the days when sea-going vessels were tiny its harbour was important not only for fishing - still carried on in a small way - but also for its trade in marble. Like so many spots on this coast Llansá has been prevented from expanding by the cliffs and steep-sided hills that flank it and make new building almost impossible. It has a tiny, rather shingly beach. But its main trade is with French visitors who pop across the frontier to enjoy its good restaurants.

Six more miles of winding clifftop road bring you to **Puerto de la Selva**, another colourful small fishing village stretching all round the sides of a small north-facing bay. If you're feeling specially energetic you can follow the two-mile track up to the ruined monastery of San Pedro de Roda, 2000 feet above sea level and with a wonderful view of the coast. The view makes you understand clearly why it's called Brava. Puerto de la Selva stages its own celebrations on 5-8 August.

Beyond it, the shore becomes so rocky and steep for nearly twenty miles that the still narrow road has to leave the sea completely. The next coastal settlement, **Cadaqués**, and tiny **Port Lligat**, a sort of westward extension but with its own craggy little bay and harbour, have long been one of this coast's most celebrated spots. They are certainly as picturesque and as colourful as anyone could want.

Olive groves cover the hillsides above the village's white-painted houses, brightened with contrasting flowers and a mass of decorative wrought-iron. While there are no beaches to speak of, there are numerous lovely small cliff-ringed coves on either side of both Cadaqués and Port Lligat. In summer however the place becomes so crowded, mainly with day excursionists, that even walking isn't always easy and getting a car in and out is a major feat. Things are even worse when the little place stages its own festival early in September.

Cadaqués first appeared in history nine centuries ago. Then its harbour was busy enough to make it a prosperous town. Between the wars it became popular with artists, and the surrealist Salvador Dali settled there. A whole gallery has been given over to his works in inland Figueras (see Excursions, below), and Cadaqués' town hall displays the works of other local residents and past residents.

You have to leave Cadaqués by the road you arrived on. After three miles or so you fork left, leaving the mountain massif of the Montaña Negra (Black Mountain), which reaches the sea six miles or so northwest at daunting Cape Creus (Cabo Creus), whose tip is out of sight to visitors unless they take a boat or climb the seven-mile track to the lighthouse.

After the fork the road drops slowly to much flatter land, marshy to the south, flanking the vast Bay of Rosas (Bahia de Rosas). **Rosas** itself is a typical old coastal settlement. But it has a spectacular sandy beach stretching southward some thirteen miles. Here there is plenty of space for development, and a huge modern resort has been built alongside the old village.

It's very attractively laid out, and includes a sizable marina, together with hotels, restaurants, shops, nightspots, and the villas and apartments that occupy most of its space. The old village's daily fish auctions (you have to be up early) and Sunday market are colourful occasions. The beach however can sometimes feel uncomfortably exposed in a high wind. The land is totally flat, with no cliffs to offer shelter. Rosas takes on a specially festive air for local celebrations in mid-August. Because the soil consists of silt carried down through the centuries by two rivers, building on much of the bay was impossible till modern techniques developed. The road, much broader now, turns inland to skirt the pleasant and ancient small town of Castelló de

Ampurias. But a seaward turning on your left leads to **Ampuriabrava**, another large and well-planned residential and tourist development. This is a really luxurious spot, with brightly-coloured villas and apartment blocks, built in what might be called imitation fishing-village style. Everything you can possibly want has been thought of - restaurants, nightclubs, golf course, tennis courts, swimming pools, riding centre, and a capacious marina.

There are ancient saltpans just north of Ampuriabrava, and the beach is within easy reach of every villa and flat. Because the surrounding land is entirely level you might imagine the scenery around the town will be dull. This isn't the case at all. Driving through the lanes inland from the Bahia de Rosas is in fact extremely enjoyable, especially in spring. The greens and colours of the area's rich vegetation are particularly pleasant and, of course, in stark contrast to the spectacular coast's cliffs and crags. It's not for nothing that the major roads in this area are lined with green on Firestone's invaluable T25 map, indicating that they're picturesque to drive along.

Some sixteen miles of easy driving bring you to the outskirts of the modern resort and ancient fishing port of **La Escala**. But first you might like to make a very short northward detour to the ruins of the ancient settlement at the Bahia de Rosas' southern end that has given its name to so much in this area. **Ampurias** derives its name from the Greek *Emporion*, their ordinary word for 'trading post' (and our word 'emporium').

Once it was an important town lying mainly on the site of the modern hamlet of Sant Marti d'Empuries - to quote its Catalan name. In 467 B.C. it was seized from the Greeks by the Carthaginians and played quite a part when Rome and Carthage fought for supremacy in the Mediterranean two centuries later. Barbarian invaders, Moors, and Normans attacked it in later years. But it lost its importance as its harbour silted up. What you see today is mainly Roman buildings whose excavation began as long ago as 1823.

La Escala itself is another old fishing harbour set in a pleasant small bay. Fishing for anchovies is still a major local occupation. But the terrain here has prevented too much modern building and there's relatively little in La Escala today that's really old. There are several hotels pretty well right in the town centre. But the beaches lie mainly south and east of the town, where the coast again becomes rocky enough to drive the road miles inland. Its private festive dates are 2-7 September.

Eight more miles of attractive scenery bring you to the old inland town of Toroella de Montgrí, from where a pleasant three-mile run takes you into flower-filled **Estartit**. This is yet another old fishing village, but one that has developed into a particularly attractive modern resort.

The sandy beach running south from the old town centre is enormous and ideal for children. The bay is well-sheltered and every sort of watersport flourishes - wind-surfing, water-skiing, scuba-diving, sailing, and swimming. Accommodation ranges from relatively small, long-established family-run hotels to vast apartment blocks. The setting is very attractive, with the craggy great Roca Maura hill towering high above beach and town and woods sweeping down to the houses and flats covering its lower slopes.

Excursions include boat trips to the Islas Medas a few miles off the coast. The shops in the old town are very appealing. The well-known Golf de Pals 18-hole course is only some fifteen miles away. It's hardly surprising that Estartit has for years been extremely popular with British holidaymakers. It manages to combine much of the best of the older Costa Brava's coastal villages with all the attractions of a modern resort. And it's an excellent centre from which to explore the surrounding countryside if that's what you enjoy. Like Port Bou it enjoys special celebrations on St James's Day, 25 July, and the three following days.

South of Estartit comes the Costa Brava's second stretch of silty alluvial land, flanked by the vast Playa de Pals, with the well-known 18-hole Golf de Pals at its southern end. But there's no possibility of making your way along the beach. Your only approach to Estartit or exit from the town is through Toroella, and there you have to return. If you want to continue south you cross the River Ter, drive some six miles to the ancient inland town of Pals, and from there another two miles to **Bagur**.

This is a very picturesque little town, built round a now-ruined 14th-century castle. It contains a number of elegant small mansions, often highly-coloured and decorated with ornate wrought-iron grilles similar to those we've seen in Cadaqués. These, people will tell you, were the homes of the *indianos* - men who made their fortunes in South America in the eighteenth century, when Catalans were for the first time allowed to trade in Spain's South American possessions. Bagur's own festival is celebrated towards the end of July.

Bagur occupies the central point of a very rocky large headland with a number of tiny resorts hidden away in secluded coves around it. **Sa Riera**, in the north, lies very close to the Golf de Pals. It has a few small hotels and some restaurants, but no real beach. To get to the coast's next settlement, **Fornells**, you have to return to Bagur. Fornells consists of little more than a few restaurants at the end of the road in a wooded cove with the sea beyond.

Aiguablava ('Blue Water') lies just beyond Fornells and is so attractive that when modern tourism first began to develop seriously after the war the Spanish government built what is still the Costa Brava's only government-run *parador*. The purpose of the paradores was to encourage international tourism in areas that were inadequately provided with hotel accommodation. It's interesting that several on the coast are in characterful places that have definitely *not* become specially popular.

If you want somewhere really 'away from it all' (with all the attendant problems of getting there, of course) you won't find many places better

27

than the Aiguablava parador. The miniature village beside it lies on one side of a tiny bay closed in by steep hills and rocky promontories and lined with lovely yellow sand. Green woods run down to the crags and caves at the water's edge. The miniature port is flanked by white-painted houses fronted by a shaded arcade. And the parador is very comfortable.

Now we have to travel inland yet again, but not quite all the way to Bagur before turning south to the much larger town of Palafrugell. This is our gateway to the attractive resort of Tamariú and the busy twin villages of Llafranch and Calella de Palafrugell.

Tamariú is often described as the Costa Brava's prettiest resort - not without reason, though not everyone agrees. It's a tiny, modest, hilly spot, situated on a small bay bounded by rocky cliffs and the hills it's built on. Its beach offers excellent swimming, but is always crowded in summer (what decent beach isn't?). It has the usual good selection of restaurants, shops, and nightspots, as well as small hotels, and is served by the passenger launches which during the season ply regularly up and down this part of the coast, where settlements now become much more frequent. A boat excursion is in fact probably the pleasantest way of visiting Tamariú if you're not staying there.

You can actually drive direct from Tamariú to Llafranch, though the signposts seem designed to prevent you from ever getting there. **Llafranch** is unlike most of what we've so far seen. It boasts a much-appreciated small beach, ending in cliffs or crags at either end and flanked by a palm-lined esplanade. It's a popular spot, which never seems to be merely moderately full of visitors. New hotels have been built on the not-too-steep slopes above it. As at neighbouring Calella, entertainment is mostly simple and quiet - which means there are plenty of bars around the waterfront and elsewhere, where you can sit and be happy. Llafranch and Calella are both very popular with holidaying Spaniards.

Calella de Palafrugell can reasonably be called Llafranch's twin because, when viewed from the sea (an excellent place to see them from), they look like one town. They're often treated as a single unit. Actually, however, they're separated by a small rocky headland which prevents you walking along the shore. Until recently, you had to go quite a way inland to get from one to the other.

Like Llafranch, Calella is essentially a quiet, peaceable, and very attractive spot. A lot of its little fishermen's houses have been brightly painted and modernised or even totally rebuilt as holiday accommodation. Its beaches are shingly rather than sandy, and set in sheltered coves, with woods covering the crags and cliffs beyond. In summer its shops and restaurants and bars are extremely busy without being noisy or boisterous. Cape Roig (Cabo Roig), a little further south (you get there by a narrow direct road) is backed by another of this coast's regions of wild, deserted, roadless clifftop stretches.

At the same time however Calella

(like Llafranch and Tamariú) makes a very good excursion base. The attractive provincial capital Gerona is barely thirty miles away. A long day out takes you to Barcelona in one direction and the Pyrenees and inland Catalonia in others. And there are regular boat trips up and down a particularly attractive stretch of coast, with opportunities to visit a whole array of other resorts.

Once again, on leaving Calella we have to drive a couple of miles inland to Palafrugell and turn south over gentle hills for the five or six miles to **Palamós**. Now we've come to a rather different sort of place. Palamós is a working town, with a fair amount of mainly small-scale industry. Indeed, it's the modern headquarters of the once-important local cork factories. That however hasn't prevented a certain degree of tourist development, though the beach on the town's northern side is pretty tiny. The seafront promenade is attractive, and the town has some pleasant fish restaurants which use the local catches. It mounts its own special festivities on 24-26 June.

Five miles of mainly flat, built-up road bring you to **Playa de Aro**, one of the region's busiest resorts. Its main appeal is provided by a curving beach nearly a mile long. Its streets have been lined with pines. There are lots of pleasant villas and, usually a few minutes away from the sea because they came later in Playa de Aro's development, a number of modern hotels. Visitors of many nationalities find it a very attractive place for holidays. Its festive dates come in late July.

Its character seems very different

from Llafranch and Calella de Palafrugell, which are themselves decidedly busy spots compared with, say, Aiguablava. Playa de Aro however has the sort of obvious energy and bustle we haven't met on this coast's more northerly stretch. Needless to say, it's well provided with discos and nightspots, as well as shops, restaurants, and bars.

Our next resort, **S'Agaró**, provides another sudden total contrast. It consists of a very peaceful, totally secluded, privately-owned estate on a headland just south of Playa de Aro. It boasts a single very luxurious hotel and a large number of villas. The owner personally approved the design of every building erected there. Non-residents aren't admitted.

It's only a stone-throw - admittedly over the top of a bit of a hill - to one of the long-popular spots on the Costa Brava, **San Feliú de Guixols** or, to give it its Catalan name, **Sant Felíu**. Note where the accent is written. That tells you where the word stress falls.

In summer San Feliú is full of visitors. In autumn, when the visitors leave, you realise that the town has a very vigorous life of its own, almost totally separated from tourism. Its narrow streets, closed in by hillsides ending in cliffs, and its small, shingly beach and harbour are as colourful as ever. You can still enjoy a stroll on the cliffs and a walk along the tree-lined seafront promenade. Or a climb up the southern hillsides to the Eremita de Sant Elm, the Hermitage of the holy man the Spaniards call San Telmo and British sailors have always known as St Elmo (he was held to be responsible for the light given by electricity discharging from the tips of yardarms and masts - St Elmo's Fire).

The colourful evening **paseo**, when everyone (especially the younger folk) turns out to stroll up and down the promenade by the sea will have stopped. But that's because the summer's heat ends pretty abruptly here as elsewhere on the Costa Brava. The thermometer stays fairly high. But cool mountain winds make it less pleasant out of doors.

San Feliú was once the centre of the region's previously flourishing cork industry. It still boasts the Costa Brava's only major bullring. It was the first of this coast's larger settlements to become popular with foreigners, and it has a number of large houses where major cork manufacturers once made their homes. One of them, the Casa Rovira in the Calle de San Amancio, is now run as an excellent and extremely reasonable guesthouse by the trilingual widow of a British journalist who became famous for his reporting of the Spanish Civil War, helped by her son James. Patricia Langdon-Davies was much younger than her husband. But like him she loves Spain and is a seemingly limitless mine of information. She's equally at home in Spanish, English, and Catalan. The same applies to her son.

The Santa Cristina Golf Club, located at **Santa Cristina de Aro** five miles inland from San Feliú, enjoys a wonderfully green setting and boasts a very comfortable clubhouse, with hotels in the village nearby. Immediately south of San Feliú itself an extremely attractive corniche road takes you the fifteen miles to Tossa de Mar, one of the Costa Brava's major resorts. It gives you lovely views over the sea and down into quiet sandy coves through the pines lining the road. If you want somewhere quiet to swim or sun yourself these little bays are ideal, provided you can find somewhere to park. That's another good reason for hiring a scooter or moped rather than a car. 1-4 August are San Feliú's festival dates.

Tossa de Mar celebrates in late June. It's one of the Costa Brava's loveliest and, very understandably, most popular resorts. It lies on a long sand-and-pebble beach, backed by hills and overlooked at its southern end by the Vila Vella (Old Town), whose battlemented walls and towers hug the contours. The Old Town flourished from about the 13th century, and remains of Roman settlement have been discovered near it. Thanks to a film which featured the Vila Vella in the 1930s the town became popular with writers and artists and other international visitors between the wars. One result is that most of the hotels that were built on the hillsides a little away from the sea are small, in keeping with the number of people who could afford the luxury of foreign travel before the war.

Another of course is that Tossa has a long, well-rooted tradition of catering for tourists. The modern town is lively and colourful, with good shops and restaurants and a few nightspots and discos, yet relatively quiet. Its main attractions are the alleys and streets of the old town and the beaches in the large bay on which the town stands, the small Cala Bona to the north and the Playa del Codolar to the south. Fairly frequent buses run south to Lloret de Mar and Blanes (see below), with organised excursions further afield to Barcelona, the spectacular monastery of Montserrat, and elsewhere. Boat trips are plentiful too. And with your own hire car or scooter the scope is even wider.

At Tossa the terrain forces the still winding and hilly road inland for the twelve miles or so to Lloret de Mar, another major resort. On the way you pass the Playa de Llorell and the Playa de Canyellas, smaller beaches where quiet little modern resorts have been established.

Lloret de Mar is a lively large modern holiday settlement with a glorious sandy beach backed by an impressive long promenade. The town stands on flat ground and is mostly modern, with lots of tall buildings looking out to sea. At the bay's northern end however, in the original fishing and trading settlement, a few houses built by successful *indianos*, similar to those in Bagur, still exist. Most have been replaced or hidden by modern structures.

Lloret's main appeal however undoubtedly lies in its extremely lively modern development - its large hotels and apartment blocks, its discos, nightspots, bars, restaurants, and shops. For many years the resort has been a British favourite, especially with younger folk, and a lot of bars and restaurants offer the sort of fare you're accustomed to at home. Ironically enough, one here, plastered with notices saying: 'Tea like mother makes it', is also capable of serving, out of season, memorable purely Spanish meals. The proprietor takes the very sensible view that Spanish and British food are both equally enjoyable.

Regular buses connect the town with Tossa and Blanes and there are plenty of boat trips available. There's a full range of organised excursions going further afield as well. In the town itself the elaborate performances and procesions, including one of decorated boats to Santa Cristina south of Lloret, during the *Festa* (as the Catalans call it) of Santa Ana on 24-25 July each year have long been famous. At Corpus Christi (date variable) Lloret holds an evening procession through streets decorated with elaborate patterns of flower petals.

Should you ever feel like having a change from Lloret's continuous bustle you can go to the beach at Fanals just south of the town or to Santa Cristina immediately beyond Fanals. Or of course to the coves between Lloret and Tossa. Ideally, you'll need your own transport.

By the time we reach **Blanes**, some five miles south of Lloret, it's obvious that the coast's character has changed. Blanes lies at the foot of sloping ground in a bay lined with an excellent beach. Southward the land is flat, while rocks and low cliffs can still be seen. The town itself is sizable, full of narrow alleys and little one-way streets that make driving distinctly difficult. Its confusingly jumbled streets are filled with white-painted small houses, bars, discos, nightspots, attractive shops and, in the summer, crowds of people.

31

A wide promenade runs behind the sandy beach. There's a fascinating aquarium containing many varieties of Mediterranean fish beside the harbour. The Marimurta Botanical Gardens on the low cliffs display over 3000 plant varieties spread over several acres. They are specially popular with British visitors and excellent guidebooks are available in English.

Blanes is over a thousand years old and was originally an important fishing and shipbuilding centre. Tourism and yachting have largely taken over today, though fishing hasn't totally disappeared. The town possesses a major winery that produces what was once called Spanish 'champagne' (EEC Law forbids that today), and a large nylon factory. Regular bus and boat services connect it with coastal towns to the north. Buses run also to Barcelona, and frequent excursions visit places of interest in summer.

The high spot of Blanes' year is its *Festa Major* (Great Festival) of Santa Ana, held on 24-25 July. But it celebrates also an amusingly named Minor Great Festival, *Festa Major Petita* in Catalan and *Fiesta Mayor Pequeña* in Castilian, dedicated to San Bonoso in September.

The Costa Dorada resorts

Gerona Province and the Costa Brava end at the River Tordera's mouth some four miles south of Blanes, and the coast's character changes very markedly. Cliffs and crags and rocky coves give way to smooth level ground - and the railway, after leaving the sea near Llansá to serve Figueras and Gerona, returns to the coast. It runs pretty close to the sea in many places, often dividing the original older settlements from beaches which in some cases have to be reached by level crossings. Trains however are neither frequent nor noisy enough to cause real problems.

In another way, too, the Costa Dorada is totally different from the Costa Brava. It's not a continuous holiday area. Resorts, or at least those of international interest, are scattered about at various points. Between them you will find minor developments, mainly modern, that provide holidays for Spaniards and maybe some foreign visitors, though less frequently for Britons. Another factor is the increasing degree of industrialisation as you approach Barcelona from the north. Spots like Canet de Mar, Arenys de Mar, and Mataró, which used to receive a fair proportion of British visitors, now have very few, if any.

Malgrat is the Costa Dorada's most northerly resort. It lies barely five miles from the River Tordera's mouth, where more silt, as in the Bahia de Rosas and the Playa de Pals, is being brought down from the mountains, making soft and often marshy land that it's difficult to build on. Originally it was a small residential town with a certain amount of small-scale industry, located away from the beach. More recently a considerable amount of holiday development has taken place close to or right beside the beach, which is long and of coarse sand interspersed with a few rocky

Magulluf on Majorca

Even in October the beach is very popular.

The Costa Brava's Tossa de Mar has a history that goes back to medieval times.

La Manga del Mar Menor, on the Costa Cálida, is purely modern.

World-famous Torremolinos, on the Costa del Solo,
doesn't consist wholly of vast concrete hotels.

patches. A fine promenade now backs the beach.

Malgrat makes a good spot for a quiet holiday. The beach is spacious. There are shops and bars and British-style pubs (well, more or less), which others apart from Brits appreciate. There's tennis and horse-riding, and the weekly market is always an attraction. If you want to explore Barcelona at your leisure it's only 35 miles away to the south by trains which serve also Blanes to the north, where you can catch buses to colourful spots still further north. And there's a good choice in season of special coach and some boat excursions. I don't need to stress that transport of your own gives you an even wider choice.

Santa Susana, a couple of miles away, is a sort of appendage of Malgrat and, indeed, is often treated as being effectively part of the larger town. It's possibly a little quieter.

Pineda however, another two miles beyond Santa Susana, consists of a decidedly quiet, peaceful residential area surrounded by new tourist development. The older part has narrow, winding streets and shaded squares, with some good restaurants and a few bars and nightspots. The beach is continuous with Santa Susana's and Malgrat's, but the sand here is somewhat coarser and shelves a bit steeply, which limits watersports slightly.

This is true also of **Calella de la Costa**, another two miles or so beyond Pineda. But this resort's character is very different from both Pineda and Malgrat-Santa Susana. It's based on a tiny old town whose

narrow streets and tiny squares are fun to explore. Most of it however is modern, and it's still expanding. An excellent palm-lined promenade has been built along the beach, which doesn't usually become over-crowded, though the town itself has the feel of being active and bustling. Railway and coach excursions are the same as for Pineda and Malgrat. Calella has long attracted visitors from many nations, and it gives the impression of being a fashionable spot.

On the way to Barcelona you pass successively through San Pol de Mar (just beyond the lighthouse on the low cliffs that bound Calella's beach to the south), Canet de Mar, Arenys de Mar, Caldetas, and Mataró before coming to a string of more purely industrial towns. All, apart from San Pol, are to a minor extent still places that visitors stay at, and Arenys caters effectively for yachtsmen. Mostly however, like Badalona, our last stop before Barcelona, they're places that the Catalan capital's residents flock to at weekends and days off. If you're driving you can avoid the crowds and the very slow coastal road by taking the inland motorway.

Barcelona is described in the section outlining excursion destinations at the end of this chapter. It's a busy, surprisingly beautiful commercial, industrial, and harbour city with a number of excellent museums and other attractions very well worth visiting.

Beyond Barcelona yet another alluvial silt area at the mouth of the River Llobregat has precluded shoreline building till recent years. Barcelona's airport stands now on its southern part, with two resorts, **Gavamar** and **Casteldefells**, a little further south. Gavamar's long beach is popular with Barcelona residents on days off. It lies on mainly flat ground. Casteldefells possesses a similarly long beach. Behind the town pine-covered hills slope up to the ancient fortifications that give the town its name. There are numerous campsites nearby. But the resort itself has been largely taken over by Spanish families and relatively few foreign tourists seem to visit it now.

Sitges is reached by some fifteen miles of low corniche road. It's the Costa Dorada's largest resort and, many would say, its finest - though Salou's fans (see below) will no doubt dispute that. Its most obvious attraction is another vast sandy beach, aptly called the Playa de Oro (Golden Beach), but that's not its only fine point. Sitges manages to combine the appeal of a very old settlement built mainly on a steep hillside with that of a well-laid-out and very busy modern resort standing largely on somewhat flatter land. It possesses also a number of impressive art galleries and museums.

The old town's streets, some dating back to mediæval times, are still largely filled with flower-decked, brightly-coloured houses and tiny shops whose appeal is very different from those of the modern areas. These, close to the beach, stretch southward from the old town, with another fine tree-lined promenade beside the sea. The town began to play host to tourists long ago when comfortably-off Catalan families built themselves elegant second homes close to the old town and the beach. Some of these fine villas still exist, despite the modern tendency to high-rise development lining the actual coast.

The town's outstanding landmark is the venerable little church standing directly above the breakwater protecting the tiny old fishing harbour at the old town's edge, with a smaller beach beyond it. The church today is a museum. Inland, not far from it in the Calle del Fonollar, the Cau Ferrat Museum contains a number of paintings by El Greco, Utrillo, and other artists, as well as by Santiago Rusiñol, the painter whose house this was and who bequeathed it to the town. Ceramics and wrought iron are also displayed here. Next door, the Maricel Museum houses Rusiñol's collection of his own works and acts as annexe to the Cau Ferrat.

The Lola Anglada Collection in the Plaza General Mola behind the Town Hall (Ayuntiamento) houses an outstanding display of seventeenth, eighteenth, and nineteenth century dolls. On the edge of the old town the Casa Llopis, an elegant old house, is devoted to the furniture, paintings, musical instruments, and other contents of a comfortable nineteenth century Catalan home. It forms part of the local Museo Romántico (Romantic Museum), which includes also the Casa Paipol at Villanueva y Geltrú, five miles south of Sitges. Here you can enjoy another display of well-heeled nineteenth century Catalan living. A single ticket admits you to all three collections.

Sitges has plenty of shops catering for visitors and a good choice of restaurants and nightspots. There's an 18-hole golf course overlooking the sea at the town's southern edge. The railway and, in summer, special excursion coaches take you quickly to Barcelona and elsewhere. The town's main festival is at Corpus Christi, whose date varies, when the old town's streets are covered with flowers arranged in complicated patterns and a colourful evening procession passes over them. Earlier in the year the town hosts the annual Carnation Show - Spain's national flower. Another *festa*, lasting over 23-24 August, is devoted mainly to local folklore.

We're still thirty miles from the fine old town of Tarragona, but few places are of any great tourist interest on our way except perhaps **Villanueva y Geltrú**, which possesses a small beach as well as the branch of the provincial Romantic Museum already mentioned. Tarragona's many points of interest are outlined below, under Excursions.

Located about ten miles from Tarragona's centre, **Salou** is the Costa Dorada's most southerly resort of any importance. Its beach is a superb long stretch of fine white sand, and it's backed by a wide and attractive promenade with extensive modern tourist development beyond it. There's everything here that modern holidaymakers can imagine themselves wanting, and it naturally attracts holiday-seekers from most of Europe - and Tarragona's weekend crowds as well. If you're after a peaceful, quiet time, Salou, with its rollicking discos and nightspots, is hardly the place for you, despite its extraordinarily spacious beach, its

fine shops and many good bars and restaurants.

For all its modernity however Salou is an ancient settlement. The attractive old town lies at the beach's northern extremity, and the now tiny-seeming harbour was large enough to act as home base for the fleet with which Jaime I, King of Aragón and Catalonia, began the reconquest of Majorca from the Moors in 1230. Excursions include trips to neighbouring **Cambrils** (five miles away), a quiet fishing town with a fine sandy beach, colourful afternoon fish market, and good fish restaurants, and to Tarragona, Poblet monastery, and elsewhere.

Thirty-odd miles of mainly flat but very attractive road bring you to the Ebro delta, where the huge, fast-flowing river's silt is extending eastward into the Mediterranean at the rate of roughly thirteen yards a year. It's about the most northerly spot where rice is grown in Spain, and most of it is now a nature reserve.

The cathedral town of **Tortosa**, inland from the delta's base, was once a busy port. In 1938, during Spain's bitter Civil War, a Republican counter-attack crossed the Ebro at Tortosa but got bogged down in long-drawn trench warfare in which 150,000 died. A memorial rising from the Ebro commemorates their loss. The Costa Dorada and Tarragona Province end some twenty miles beyond the delta.

Excursions

It's not possible to say exactly what excursions are available from which resorts. There may be variations according to the season, with fewer at the beginning and end of the summer, and from one year to another. What follows is a general account of the main places you may be able to see, possibly on organised trips and certainly by hire car.

Trips to the Islas Medas from Estartit, boat trips up and down the coast at points on the Costa Brava's central northern stretch (San Feliú to Tamariú), trains to Barcelona from Malgrat-Santa Susana-Pineda, and the buses between Tossa, Lloret, and Blanes have already been mentioned. The northern Costa Brava's hinterland and the corniche between San Feliú and Lloret are well worth seeing. It remains to describe briefly a few specific destinations.

From the northern part of the Costa Brava in particular it's possible to make a longish day trip to **Perpignan** in France (if you think of hiring a car, consider the conditions for taking it over the frontier: hirers' arrangements vary). The distance seems pretty large, but the modern motorway is surprisingly fast and, with luck, the frontier queues won't be too long. And Perpignan is an ancient Catalan town well worth seeing. When Jaime I of Catalonia had expelled the Moorish invaders from Majorca in 1235 he installed one of his sons as King of Majorca with the Catalan areas north of the Pyrenees (the Roussillon and the Cerdagne) as part of his territory. Perpignan was the new king's capital.

A ring of wide boulevards marks - roughly - the line of the old walls.

Inside it the whole area is filled with alleys and narrow little streets. The main buildings that everyone wants to see however are Le Castillet, the Loge de Mer, the fine Cathedral, and the Palace of the Kings of Majorca (Palais des Rois de Majorque).

The first three all lie within a couple of hundred yards of the town's former main gate, originally a water gate spanning the Basse stream and approached by the Pont Joffre (Joffre Bridge) across the main River Têt. Le Castillet was a small fortress designed to deter attackers and also to keep the townsfolk in order. Today it houses the Casa Pairal, a museum of traditional Catalan customs and handicrafts. The Loge de Mer (Sea Lodge) was built as a maritime law court similar to the one on Palma's seafront in Majorca, where disputes involving merchants or seafaring folk were decided.

The Cathedral of St John consists of a fascinating jumble of every architectural style from twelfth century Romanesque to an eighteenth century wrought-iron belltower. On the other side of the old town, all of half a mile away (though you'll inevitably get lost in the tangle of alleyways), a fortified citadel surrounds the beautifully restored Palace of the Kings of Majorca. The original building dates from the thirteenth and fourteenth centuries, with a particularly fine double-galleried courtyard, and the surrounding fortifications from the seventeenth.

Other places of interest include the fifteenth century Law Courts (Palais de Justice) and the thirteenth century Town Hall (Hôtel de Ville).

The Musée Rigaud contains an interesting collection of Catalan primitives, thirteenth to fifteenth century Hispano-Moorish tiles, Catalan ceramics, and other items, as well as paintings by the seventeenth century artist Henri Rigaud.

Inside Spain, the provincial capital **Gerona** is an enjoyable town to spend time in, though driving in it is purgatory because of its tangle of one-way streets and its not very adequate signposting. Walking around the old town however is pure bliss. It lies on a slope to the east of the River Oñar, beside its junction with the Ter. It's full of stepped streets and narrow alleys, and its ancient buildings include the remains of Arab baths (Baños Árabes) dating from the twelfth century, as well as a very fine Cathedral begun in the fourteenth century, which you approach by a wonderful flight of seventeenth century steps. There are a number of fine old houses in the town as well.

Figueras, twenty-five miles or so north of Gerona and just off the motorway, is a place of pilgrimage for anyone who admires the artist Salvador Dali's work. The town's former theatre has been converted into an art gallery devoted wholly to him.

If you've hired a car or scooter (perhaps not a moped) and get into conversation with any of the locals they'll almost certainly urge you to spend a day touring the **Sierra del Montseny**, an extraordinary mountain range lying inland from Calella de la Costa and Barcelona. It rises to a height of over 5500 feet,

and appears from a distance to be a sort of massive dome covered with dense cork oak forests. If you've never seen cork trees before, this is a golden opportunity to discover their extraordinary bark which continuously renews itself as men strip it off. The roads however are narrow and very tortuous, and you'll certainly need a very good map. The Firestone T25 is ideal because it carries an enlargement of the Montseny range on its reverse side.

Among other useful detailed maps it offers also a sound working street plan of central **Barcelona**. This magnificent city is by far the most important and attractive of all this exciting region's excursion destinations - though you need to be warned that it can become almost unbearably hot and dusty on summer afternoons, when sensible people doze indoors and only tourists plod dedicatedly on (dolts!). It contains a great deal that you somehow don't expect to find in a large city.

In the first place it has some magnificently long, straight roads magnificent, that is, as long as you don't have to brave their traffic for too long. If you drive a car into Barcelona your best advice is to duck into the first underground car park you see - there are lots of them - and make a *very* careful note of its name and address. You'll find it much easier to continue on foot - and less tiring too despite the possible heat. Perhaps you'd be well advised to take a coach excursion first and reserve your real exploration of the city for a second visit.

Where do you start? Down by the

quay perhaps, at the Plaza Puerta de la Paz (Peace Gate Square), close to where the ferries for Majorca, Menorca, and Ibiza leave. The square's dominated by a column commemorating Christopher Columbus (Cristóbal Colón in Spanish). A replica of his ship, the Santa Maria, is moored opposite. The famous succession of leafy broad avenues always known as the Ramblas (*rambla* means avenue) leads out of the square. With their souvenir kiosks, superb flower stalls, news stands where you can buy British and other newspapers and magazines, and innumerable cafés they make up a fascinatingly popular shopping area.

Half way up the Ramblas the Calle Fernando takes you off to the right, into the Plaza San Jaime (St James Square) and the equally famous Barrio Gótico (Gothic Quarter) which - surprise! surprise! - contains a mass of impressive Gothic buildings.

The fifteenth century Town Hall stands on your right as you enter the Plaza San Jaime, though its facade on this side is modern. The side facing the Calle de la Ciudad is original. So is one of the courtyards. The other contains richly ornate reliefs of the type called plateresque, which evolved during Spain's sixteenth century Golden Era. The name comes from the word for silversmith (*platero*) because the style of carving resembles silversmith's work.

The fifteenth century building on the square's other side now houses the Generalitat, Catalonia's regional assembly, abolished in 1939 at the end of the disastrous Civil War and

restored in 1977. Its courtyard, tower, and chapel are specially striking. The Cathedral and its cloisters, opposite the further end of the Generalitat's main front, date mainly from the thirteenth to fifteenth centuries, though the facade and spire are modern. The Cathedral, its cloisters, and its museum are worth an hour's investigation. Remains of a Visigoth palace, a fourth century Christian basilica, and a temple dedicated to the Roman Emperor Augustus have been found under the Cathedral. The Barrio Gótico was in fact the site of the Roman settlement.

When you can tear yourself away from the Gothic Quarter try going back to the Ramblas and crossing them into what is called the Barrio Chino (Chinese Quarter), though no one quite knows why. It's a cosmopolitan area of cheap bars, restaurants, and nightclubs reminiscent, in a way, of London's Soho.

The Ramblas' inland end takes you into the large Plaza de Cataluña (Catalonia Square), one of the town's main shopping centres. From the Plaza de Cataluña there's a view up the Avenida Reina Maria Cristina towards Montjuich hill, directly south of our starting-point, that's specially fine on evenings when the fountains are lit up. And Montjuich itself is another must.

Apart from a large sports stadium, Montjuich is home to three important museums - the Museum of Catalan Art (Museo de Arte de Cataluña), housed in the former National Exhibitions Palace (Palácio Nacional de Exposiciones); the Miró

Foundation; and the Pueblo Español (Spanish Village).

The Museum of Catalan Art houses an important collection of Catalan primitives up to the fifteenth century, as well as fine frescos and excellent examples of paintings by fifteenth to eighteenth century Spanish artists, such as Ribera, Velasquez, and Zurbarán. The Miró Collection displays works not only by Miró but also by other moderns.

It's the Pueblo Español however that attracts absolutely every visitor to Montjuich. Built originally for Barcelona's 1929 International Exhibition it consists of reconstructions of streets and squares containing examples of typical architecture drawn from all Spain - Spain in a nutshell, if you like, and a wonderful sampler for travels in the rest of the country. On 23 and 29 June and 24 September the Pueblo Español is illuminated and *en fête*.

Other important museums and art galleries elsewhere in the city include the Picasso Museum, located in the heart of the old town in a sixteenth century aristocratic house at 15 Calle Moncada. Most of the collection consists of drawings, engravings and watercolours. But there are also a number of outstanding paintings, including the very famous Harlequin.

For many visitors Barcelona's most memorable monument is the extraordinary Church of the Holy Family (Sagrada Familia). It stands at the end of the Avenida de Gaudí, whose name commemorates the architect. Antonio Gaudí worked on the church himself from 1884 on.

He began in conventional Neo-Gothic and then developed the idiosyncratic welter of imaginative decoration that we see today. Unfortunately, he was run over by a tram and killed in 1926. Completing his building in the 1940s was extremely difficult because he had left no comprehensible drawings.

The city becomes pretty impossible on St George's Day, 23 April. St George is Catalonia's patron saint. The June Trade Fair is pretty busy too.

Before you desert the city however you ought to experience driving up the enormously long Avenida del Generalísimo Franco which cuts across the nineteenth century town's grid pattern of streets and is always referred to as the *Diagonal* as a result. And then go to the top of the hill called Tibidabo (1745 feet: to the west) for the magnificent view over the city.

Tarragona may seem rather small beer after Barcelona. But it's a major port, large commercial and industrial centre, and provincial capital, as well as one of Spain's many impressive great cities. To really enjoy it however you need not only to be something of both archaeologist and ancient historian, but also to use some sort of really erudite handbook that explains everything in detail. Unfortunately no such book seems to exist.

That's a pity. Extant parts of Tarragona's city walls are of what's called 'cyclopean' construction - gigantic prehistoric stone blocks put in position thousands of years ago no one knows how. The Romans conquered the city in 218 BC and made it one of the loveliest and most elegant Roman cities in Spain. A lot of their work can still be seen, including remains two miles away of an aqueduct that brought water to the town.

Set right in the heart of the mediæval city's narrow streets the Cathedral was built on top of a Roman Temple of Jupiter. Its unusually large cloisters show clear Moorish influence. Close to the sea you can visit the remains of an arena where a number of leading Christians were burned in 259 AD. And you can find plenty of shops to enjoy not only around the Cathedral but also in the city's two main modern thoroughfares, the Rambla de San Carlos and the Rambla del Generalísimo. Tarragona's annual high spot is the festivities that last from 8 to 19 August.

Visiting old monasteries isn't everyone's cup of tea. For the most part they don't mean a lot except to people who really understand their spirit and history or are particularly attracted by their architecture. **Montserrat** however is a bit different. Its location among towering rocky mountains, sheer cliffs, and high crag pinnacles alone makes the visit memorable. Many of the roads around it are spectacular in the extreme, and you get to the top of some neighbouring mountain peaks by cable car and funicular.

Montserrat's sumptuous buildings are relatively modern, constructed after French troops had destroyed almost totally the original tenth century foundation in 1812. But Montserrat is memorable for its history rather than its present architecture. In particular, it deserves a place of special honour with anyone who enjoys music. Its choir school, run on lines similar to those of English Cathedrals, has been famous since the thirteenth century, and is still regarded as outstanding for its singing of Gregorian chant. The school's many famous pupils include the composer Fernando Sor (1778-1839), very well known to every classical guitarist, whose masses are also still regularly sung at Montserrat.

Other monasteries in mountain locations visited by organised excursions include **Poblet**, some thirty miles inland from Tarragona, and **San Cugat**, barely twenty miles from Barcelona.

A final word about venturing into the Spanish countryside on your own, whether by personal transport or on some public conveyance. Too many Britons are ridiculously worried about not talking the local language. The simple fact is that you don't need to. No one expects you to, and they're completely geared to coping. So stop worrying.

5.   Majorca, Menorca, Ibiza and Formentera

The four Balearic Islands (Islas Baleares in Spanish) and attendant minor islets constitute one of the world's busiest concentrations of tourist activity. Holidaymakers flock to them, and particularly to Majorca (Mallorca in Spanish), from every corner of Europe, from North America, and even from Japan and other Oriental countries. Brits who've never been there make the usual snide remarks. But the Balearics' tourist popularity never diminishes, and many who know the islands well go back time after time to their favourite island and their favourite resort. Explaining this solid attraction however isn't easy. Maybe it's something to do with the indefinable appeal that islands so often exercise and which defies analysis.

The Balearics lie between sixty and ninety miles from the Spanish coast, to which they're linked by car ferries and air services, mainly from Barcelona. They constitute a separate Spanish province whose capital is Palma de Mallorca. Yet in a number of very apparent ways they're different from Spain.

For the three centuries up to 1230 they were occupied by Arab-Islamic Moorish invaders. We usually call them 'Moorish' because their main territory was Morocco and their blood was not pure Arab but plentifully mixed with that of the North African Berbers who seem to have occupied their present homes since time immemorial.

The Moors were driven out of the islands 750 years ago by King Jaime I of Catalonia. But clear traces of their influence can still be seen in, for instance, the irrigation system that keeps much of Majorca fertile. It consists of a network of channels fed from cisterns that water's pumped into. Except that windmills and sometimes other pumps have replaced Arab waterwheels (*norias*), worked by humans or animals (donkeys or mules), nothing has changed since the invaders built the system.

Place-names beginning with Al- and Ben- or Bin-, especially common on Menorca, are relics of Arabic names. Many fortifications, including those of Alcudia, the walls around Palma's old town, and a number of churches clearly built as much for defence as for worship date from the days when attacks from the sea by corsairs (as Moorish raiders from Islamic North Africa were called) were regular events. The last took place in 1830. Menorca's strange prehistoric stone *talayots* and *navetas*, heroic in size and of unknown date and origin, are also not found in Spain or elsewhere.

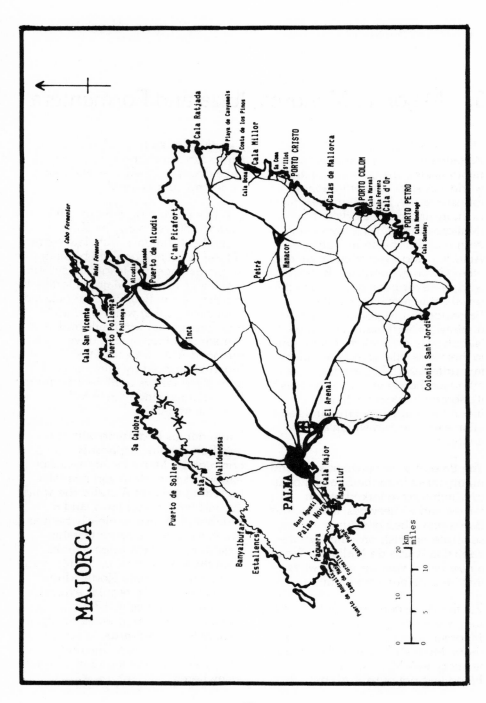

MAJORCA

In other respects the islands today have more in common with other Mediterranean islands such as Corsica, Sicily, and Malta than with mainland Spain. Social and economic problems in particular are very similar, as studies centred at the University of Corsica show very clearly. Until very recently there was far more interchange of ideas as well as commerce inside the Mediterranean basin than people today seem to realise - between islands that now lack any form of intercommunication, as well as between mainland points and mainland and islands. The Balearics share more strongly in this 'Mediterranean' connection than in any purely Spanish character.

Further, the islands' language is Catalan rather than the Castilian which we call Spanish. As on the Costa Brava, place-names come in two forms - San Agustin, for instance, and Sant Agusti are the same place. Especially on Majorca, if you try to talk 'Spanish' in remote villages people will just stare at you.

Finally, while the Costa Brava, thanks to chill winds blowing off the inland mountains, becomes quickly cool when summer ends, the Balearic islands can be very mild (but not invariably) in even the depth of winter.Ibiza's temperatures can top 70° in mid-January. At the same time the winds blowing out of a clear blue sky can be devastating, and to enjoy the sun you need very sheltered spots. This wind, coming from the north, is actually the *mistral* that blows so fiercely in southern France. When it reaches the Balearics its strength seems unabated. But it isn't cold.

MAJORCA AND ITS RESORTS

Majorca's anything but the single unit you'd imagine it to be from the way some people - especially critics who don't know the place - talk about it. For holiday purposes its settlements and resorts can be broken down into seven categories.

First come the 'lively' large resorts of El Arenal and Magalluf. **Second**, a set of 'medium' or 'mixed' resorts - holiday spots that are neither too spirited nor too quiet and are sometimes located in corners that are very attractive indeed. **Third** place goes to a number of decidedly quiet spots, some ideal for families with young children, some for young and not so young couples who want to be mainly on their own, and some just plain remote.

Fourth come 'working' resorts - towns that have a busy life of their own and are also pleasant holiday spots. In **fifth** place there's the totally unique west coast, spread picturesquely along the lower edges of mountains sloping steeply to the sea. **Sixth** come the quiet inland towns and villages that have a life of their own almost totally separate from tourism (except that they supply vegetables and fruit and sometimes some staff to the tourist hotels). They aren't really resorts, though some are regular excursion destinations.

Finally, **seventh**, there's the fine large provincial capital, Palma, decidedly Spanish in its nineteenth century and modern quarters, but Catalan and Mallorquín, and in some corners Moorish, in its mediæval nucleus. This is the order used here for describing the island.

Large and lively

Majorca's two liveliest resorts, El Arenal and Magalluf, are located east and west respectively of Palma, the island's large and splendid capital. Both have magnificent beaches, but in other respects are very different.

El Arenal is the older of the two. It lies on totally flat land fronted by a superlative three miles of sandy beach, which (strictly speaking) it shares with Las Maravillas and C'an Pastilla, though you can't easily tell where one begins and the other ends. Though Majorca's enormously busy airport is equidistant from El Arenal and Palma - and they're barely 10 miles apart - it doesn't seem to cause much disturbance in El Arenal. The flight paths certainly don't pass over the town. Or maybe you just never notice the noise.

The beach is backed by a road, palm-lined in places, with endless hotels (most of them small), bars, shops, discos, restaurants, snackbars and English-style pubs along its further side. You'll see names like the Robin Hood, the Hole in the Wall, and Ye Olde Canary Inn (not really British?). Certain brands of British beer may also be well advertised - even though you'll also find a lot of people drinking lemonade or un-British coke, while many of the small restaurants clearly cater specially for individual nationalities - British in one, Germans in another, Swedes in a third, and so on.

One thing that's striking is the way the promenade always seems to be crowded, and the tremendous feeling of energy the place gives off.

Many tour operators maintain that it's an ideal spot for 16-28 year olds. When you're there however it's obvious that people of all ages can be found at El Arenal, including numerous families with young children. And they belong to every conceivable nationality, including Spaniards.

El Arenal's side streets are filled largely with the same mixture of hotels, bars, shops, restaurants, etc as the seafront. Though the crowds naturally aren't as large here, the hotels are often vast. The older hotels are usually the smaller ones right on the seafront or close to it. The newer and larger may be a few minutes' walk from the sea, but never more than very few. Throughout El Arenal, though the resort spreads for miles along the coast, there's an endless choice of places to go and things to do. The really smart place to foregather is the Yacht Club (Club Náutico) at the beach's eastern (more accurately southeastern) end. But you have to be a member, or a member's guest, to get in. But you'll find places you like wherever your hotel's located.

A word about the place-names. El Arenal is sometimes, especially in British tour operators' brochures, called just Arenal and I've even seen Arenals. C'an Pastilla was originally a separate village, with its own attractive small harbour, at the beach's western end. It's still semi-separate and rather more peaceful than the place most folk call El Arenal. The beach and the settlement backing it are both sometimes known as the Playa de Palma and sometimes even, as on the Firestone T26 map, the Playas de Mallorca (Beaches of Majorca), as though it weren't one long stretch of sand.

The name Las Maravillas seems to have been abandoned in recent years. It appears that originally there was a small village called El Arenal at the end of these three miles of sand close to the present Yacht Club, one at the beach's opposite end still called C'an Pastilla, and a development between them known for a time either as Las Maravillas or as Playa de Palma or Playas de Mallorca.

Magalluf (Magaluf in Spanish) has been developed much more recently than El Arenal. It's about the same distance from the centre of Palma, and is most easily reached by the motorway. The old road, often rather narrow and slow, is built-up the whole way and passes through a series of smaller resorts, none of which has a beach that is even vaguely comparable with Magalluf's vast sweep of gleaming sand. This magnificent beach was neglected till relatively recently simply because there was no infrastructure of roads, water and electricity supply, sewage, and so on near it.

That has changed with a vengeance. Magalluf has a vast number of often extremely large, mostly very well-planned and well-equipped modern hotels, nearly all set back a little from the shore, and surrounded by pinewoods. Broad main streets are lined with souvenir kiosks, shops, restaurants, bars, English-style pubs (Coach and Horses, Britannia, etc), discos and nightclubs. In summer and even as late as October everything seems always to be crowded. It's about as busy and lively a resort as you could ever imagine. The only thing it lacks - if you can call it a lack - is a seafront promenade.

Excursions naturally go to every part of the island. There are frequent and cheap buses to Palma. Boat trips also operate to Palma and elsewhere, and there are facilities both for watersports and for things like tennis. Like El Arenal, it's an excellent starting-point for car or scooter tours.

Magalluf's huge beach is flat, but is separated from the smaller beaches of Palma Nova (on the Palma side) by a wide, rocky headland. Houses cover this promontory, so that no obvious boundary exists between the two places. I find it difficult however to regard them as a single resort.

Not too large and not too quiet

Palma Nova was developed much earlier than Magalluf, and seems to me to be quite different in character. In fact, it's really one of the island's 'medium' resorts, not too lively but by no means quiet. Hotels, large blocks of holiday flats, shops and everything else have been packed in around a shore that is mostly rocky, though with a number of sandy and relatively quiet beaches. Not so many years ago Palma Nova was basically an up-market, rather exclusive place. But it's much more of a popular resort today.

As with Magalluf, you need to look a little closely at what your brochures say to discover exactly where your hotel is and how far away from the beach. Distances in Palma Nova aren't large. But the place is pretty heavily built up and is a trifle hilly - which is fine if you like walking, but not so good if you don't. Excursions, needless to say, go virtually everywhere worth seeing on the island and there are frequent buses to Palma.

Three of Majorca's other 'medium' resorts enjoy situations overlooking the north coast's two superb stretches of sand. They are C'an Picafort, Puerto Pollença (Pollensa in Spanish), and Puerto de Alcudia (often mistakenly called Alcudia which, strictly speaking, is the fortified old town a mile inland that still retains much of its walls). Largely because of the huge sandy beaches all three resorts are excellent for families with young children.

C'an Picafort stands at the eastern end of the Bahia de Alcudia's glorious five-mile stretch of sand. The town's mostly modern. It stands on flat ground and is designed almost wholly for holidaymakers. It certainly provides very effectively for them, though the hotels aren't by any means strung along the seafront. Some are situated a little beyond the tiny old town, which is itself just beyond the beach's eastern end.

Puerto de Alcudia occupies the same beach's western end. If you look at most maps you'll be tempted to ask why hotels and resorts aren't spread all along the beach's landward side. The answer's simple, and clearly shown on the Firestone T26. The land behind the beach's central part is marshy and has for centuries been given over to extensive saltpans - areas where sea water is allowed first to flow into shallow troughs and then to evaporate until the remaining salt can be scooped out and sold. This northern part of Majorca is also well known for its birdwatching, with a fine selection of waterfowl.

As its name suggests, Puerto de Alcudia is a port. Fishing is still actively carried on, and the quayside is always an attractive corner in which to stand and stare. The resort area is however rather separated from the town's non-tourist activities. Once again, the development is nearly all modern, and carefully planned to provide everything that holidaymakers intent on enjoying the Mediterranean sun will want. One of this area's extra attractions is its tremendous feeling of openness. You seem to have the whole sky stretching over your head. The vast expanse of peaceful sea and the backdrop of mountains reinforces the impression. That's obviously true everywhere. But for some reason you become very conscious of it on this bit of Majorca's coast.

Because of their position close to the island's northern tip, Puerto de Alcudia and the two nearby resorts of C'an Picafort and Puerto Pollença are maybe a shade less well situated for excursions to some parts of Majorca than places closer to Palma, from which all the fast roads radiate. They make up for this however by having the spectacular 600 foot high vertical cliffs of Cabo (Cape) Formentor, the island's extreme northern tip, an acceptable distance away. The road to the cape, which goes via Puerto Pollença, is however very tough driving.

There are one or two hotels further north on the Bay of Alcudia's western side at **Aucanada**, just outside Puerto de Alcudia. They share many of Puerto de Alcudia's advantages. Views from them however are rather spoiled by a large power station right on the coast.

Puerto Pollença nestles, like Puerto de Alcudia, under the hills at the western or, more accurately, northwestern end of another fine stretch of sand, this time divided into a number of beaches with a sprinkling of pebbles strung out along the vast Bahia de Pollença. The mountains at the base of fifteen mile long Cabo Formentor make a wonderful backdrop to the west - and provide good shelter from much of the wind too, making windsurfing and water-skiing that much pleasanter. The harbour's always attractive to watch. The old town of Pollença, roughly three miles inland, is attractive to wander in, too. Above it stands a calvary reached by 365 steps. Puerto de Pollença's hotels have virtually all been built relatively recently in a resort area added to the old town and planned to provide all the holiday facilities international visitors expect.

For the next 'medium' resort we have to jump to **Paguera**, beyond Magalluf, close to Majorca's extreme southwestern point. Woods and low mountains form the backdrop here, and the resort's spread along the flatter land beside two sand- and-shingle beaches separated by a low rocky promontory. Some of the hotels stand on slightly higher ground a little way inland, but others are right on the shore. To a greater extent than most of the resorts we have so far considered Paguera is a mixture of old and new towns.

When the people living on Majorca were forced to wrest a living from the land and from fishing they didn't think the beaches were much use to them. Perhaps that was lucky. Paguera's one of many places where there has been plenty of room for modern development beside the older settlement. While Paguera makes a rather more peaceful impression than, say, Magalluf, which is barely ten miles away, it provides all essential holiday entertainment, and adds some restaurants that bring people all the way from Palma.

Our next 'medium' resort is completely different. It's totally modern and located in the northern half of the remote-seeming, heavily indented east coast. Resorts along this coast all seem remote because they have no real main roads leading to them. They're served by a road running roughly parallel to the shore, but up to three miles inland. And the majority of them lie on dead-end turnings off this road. **Cala Millor** is a little different in that it's big enough to have two link roads and to be connected also across a headland to the much smaller and quieter Cala Bona to the north. Cala Bona is described below.

Cala Millor possesses a mile of gently-curving, gently-sloping sand and is totally modern. It has been well laid out, with attractive stretches of palms and greenery behind the beach. There are a lot of villas and apartment blocks, which mix single-storey and high-rise quite effectively, as well as hotels, restaurants, discos, shops and so on in the town. A lot of flowers too. Because little Cala Bona is its only neighbour the town provides its own entertainment. Though large, the beach's very gentle slope makes it specially safe for young children.

Cala d'Or lies close to the east coast's further end. It's a very attractive, out-of-the-way modern holiday settlement that extends over a number of small coves, each with its beach of fine sand, forming part of a larger bay. Everything in Cala d'Or's modern. The choice of hotels is varied. There are plenty of attractive bars and restaurants, and also discos, which become very lively in the evenings. Excellent dress and jewellery shops cater well for visitors. The headlands separating the coves and the countryside round about are all covered with wonderful pinewoods, and at the season's height the beaches become very crowded. Cala d'Or makes up a little world apart, with a trendy life of its own that's anything but quiet.

Quiet and peaceful

Now we pass to Majorca's many small quiet seaside corners. In their way they're almost as varied as the rest of the island. Do you want somewhere that's just remote? Somewhere that gives the feeling of being ideal for young couples? For couples that maybe aren't quite so young? Somewhere that families with young children can really enjoy because they're quiet and

traffic-free? Majorca has them all - and many are strung along its eastern coast.

Our best plan is probably to start at the eastern coast's northern end and summarise each little place's character, omitting Cala Ratjada, which falls into the 'working' resort category and Cala d'Or and Cala Millor, already dealt with.

Playa de Canyamels is the first developed resort south of Cala Ratjada, though others are projected for the future. It's very small, with a single hotel and a small sandy beach backed by very attractive pinewoods on fairly flat land. It's reached by a dead-end road.

Costa de los Pinos, barely three miles south as the crows fly but requiring a thirteen-mile drive by road, aims at being very luxurious. The pinewoods which give it its name are magnificent. It's extremely well provided with tennis courts, and it was reported some years ago that its nine-hole golf course was to be extended to eighteen holes, though that seems not to have been done. It possesses one very comfortable hotel and a smallish sandy beach.

For once, you can actually go direct along the coast to **Cala Bona**, about four miles. Cala Bona has a pleasant old fishing harbour at the end of a small bay and two beaches made from imported sand. There have been hotels here for twenty years and they're comfortably integrated into the little town's ordinary life. The seafront in fact is lined with hotels, restaurants, bars, and shops. Nightlife is not much emphasised, but you can always wander over to Cala Millor, a short taxi ride or a twenty-minute walk to the south. Cala Millor was dealt with above.

From Cala Bona or Cala Millor you've a seven or eight mile drive or a half-hour's slightly hilly but pleasant walking to reach the up-and-coming new resort of **Sa Coma** - so up-and-coming that a dual-carriageway approach from the parallel coast road was almost the first thing built. Not a lot has followed it so far - just some apartments, one or two shops, and an enterprising small bar on the beach. But if it's real peace and seclusion you're after, along with a pleasant sandy beach, you could do a great deal worse.

S'Illot, still further south and separated by a rocky promontory, is only marginally more advanced. It has a small sandy beach, a hotel, a few shops, a bar or two, and facilities for things like cycle hire and horse-riding, as well as some excursions.

The next settlement, after a three-mile stretch of totally inaccessible, rocky coast, is **Porto Cristo**. It's a nearly landlocked harbour with attractive yachting possibilities, lying at the foot of steep hills. It's a very attractive spot indeed, with a narrow sandy beach on the bay's inner side. Accommodation is fairly limited, and there's no space to build large modern hotels. If you like the Spanish atmosphere Porto Cristo's a very pleasant spot to visit.

A full twelve miles separate it from the next resort, the newly developed and still developing **Calas de Mallorca**. The hotels here stand on the top of a wide rocky headland, with small sandy beaches in coves on either side. Some shops, a restaurant or two, and a few bars make up the entire resort. Buses run into Porto Cristo, and if you start early you can get into Palma and back inside the day.

There are more developments near Calas de Mallorca to the south, but none of international appeal. The next place of interest is **Porto Colom**, and a very attractive spot it is too. It lies in a steep-sided, almost totally landlocked large bay. Its harbour contains a wonderful collection of craft, including a number of small fishing boats. The bay's shore is totally built up. The hotels stand on a headland to the south or overlook the sandy Cala Marsal directly south of Porto Colom proper. Excursion possibilities aren't enormous.

Cala Marsal (or **Marçal**) is this spot's real resort area. It's a sort of tiny suburb of Porto Colom, tucked into a little cove with a small, attractive sandy beach that's very suitable for small children.

Cala Ferrera is virtually a little northern suburb of Cala d'Or, which has been dealt with above. It has its own beach set in its own sandy little cove. It's a decidedly quiet and peaceful spot.

A colourful, winding road takes you the four miles or so from Cala Ferrera through Cala d'Or to **Porto Petro**, another lovely deep creek similar to Porto Cristo's and Porto Colom's. Like them the village is surrounded by steep hills. But there's no beach - just rocks all round the bay. It's a friendly little spot, and worth visiting, but not a place to stay in. **Cala Mondragó**, directly south of Porto Petro, is however an enchanting spot if all you want is sun and sand and sea and peace. Apart from accommodation it contains nothing more than a shop, a few bars, and a sandy beach that's ideal for small children.

The last little creek on the east coast is also delightful. **Cala Santayani** takes its name from the town of Santanyi (St Anne), three miles inland. Its lovely sand beach is roughly two hundred yards wide and rather deeper than that. It shelves very gently into very sheltered water. White-painted hotels stand on the steep-sided little headlands around the beach, with everything wrapped in scented pinewoods. There's no traffic, and it's hard to imagine a more attractive spot for young children and their parents.

South of Cala Santanyi the east coast hills finally disappear and the land becomes very flat and in places marshy. Significantly, the cape that separates the east coast from the south is called Cabo de Salines (Saltpan Cape). There are in fact flourishing saltpans eight or nine miles further on, west of the cape. But before we reach them we come to another very quiet, as yet little developed new resort - **Colonia Sant Jordi**. There's a village with this name that has a fishing harbour and two sandy beaches, with some of the hotels close to them. But the main development is clearly destined for the magnificent huge sandy beach of Es Trench, west of the village. It has the saltpans inland, and the hotels are already spreading towards it on the headland

separating village and Es Trench beach.

While there's nothing of special interest for foreign visitors along the rest of the south coast till you get back to El Arenal, there are some pretty quiet urban resorts of a rather different kind - well, moderately quiet - west of Palma that must be mentioned.

Cala Major (Mayor in Spanish), **Sant Agusti**, and **Illetas** adjoin each other in shallow, mostly rock-lined bays immediately beyond the busy harbour area on Palma's western edge. They're rather hemmed in between main road and shore, and the entire area tends to be pretty heavily built up. But there are three stretches of sandy beach and areas of pinewoods. It's in Cala Mayor that the Spanish royal family has their summer residence, and it was here that Prince Charles and Princess Diana once spent a holiday.

These resorts are by no means without younger visitors. And they're by no means remote, unlike many more recently developed east coast resorts. They give the impression however that their main appeal is to rather older folk, perhaps because people feel that they're close to Palma and all its fine shops and restaurants. Because of their nearness to Palma and its radiating main roads these places are also specially suitable for hire-car and scooter excursions. But ask about hotel parking before you book.

Four more quiet resorts on this part of the coast must be dealt with before we turn to our so-called 'working' resorts.

Cala Viña (or Vinya or Viñas) is a sort of southern outlier to Magalluf, with a tiny beach of its own and the big resort very close. **Santa Ponça** (or Ponsa) is reached by a fork from the main road a few miles beyond Magalluf. It's spread out around quite a large bay, lined with low rocks, rugged cliffs, and pinewoods. A lot of the accommodation is in self-catering apartments, with the bay's two sandy beaches within easy walking distance. Virtually all the hotels and apartment blocks have their own swimming pools, and a lot of people do their sunbathing without bothering to go to the beach at all. If you want a livelier time Magalluf can be reached very easily by bus.

Fornells, about ten miles further on from Santa Ponça, is an enchanting little steep-sided cove, very attractively laid out. There are hotels to the south and villas on the opposite side, with a small sandy beach in the middle. But the rocky shoreline rises fast from the sea, you can get a lot of exercise without having to walk very far, and a lot of sun by simply sitting on the terrace outside your hotel. When you're old enough to want to sit in the sun doing nothing think about drifting off to Fornells.

Or maybe to **Camp de Mar**, only three or four miles further on. It has a pleasant small sandy beach, with a hotel at one end of it, some holiday flats, and a few shops and restaurants - and that's about all. Since it's not much more than thirty miles from Palma it seems extraordinary that it hasn't been much more intensively developed. If you want a little rush and bustle you can go into Paguera (about six

miles) or venture as far afield as Magalluf or even Palma.

Work and tourism mixed

Holiday spots where people mix catering for visitors equally with carrying on an ordinary working life have a special sort of appeal, especially if they're set in attractive surroundings. Majorca has three such spots.

The first is little **Puerto de Andraitx**, only a few miles from Camp de Mar by a lovely mountain road. As the name implies, it's the harbour serving the small mountain town of Andraitx, some three miles inland, and all the farms which in bygone days would have bought supplies in Andraitx and sold their surplus produce there. The harbour lies at the base of a deep bay, lined with cliffs and pinewoods. Lots of fine large yachts use the harbour, and there are working boats in it too. The town has some hotels and a reasonable number of restaurants, but not a lot in the way of special tourist entertainment. Its beach is small, but adequate. The setting however is enchanting. And the view when a blazing red setting sun's dropping fast into the sea exactly opposite the bay's mouth is unforgettable.

The second 'working' resort lacks Puerto de Andraitx's beauty, but is very attractive in a different way. It's **Cala Ratjada**, right at the island's northeastern tip, about as far from Puerto de Andraitx as you can get. Cala Ratjada has a busy and very colourful harbour, filled with fishing boats and yachts and people who seem perpetually pleased to see visitors. There are sandy beaches in pleasant bays on either side of the town, and hotels built, for the most part a little away from the centre. Self-catering apartments are also available, and there's a good choice of restaurants. Some of them specialise in fish dishes made from each morning's catch.

Cala Ratjada's pretty remote. You approach it through the little town of Capdepera, dominated by the ruins of an impressive castle and set among largely bare hills rising to over a thousand feet. If you're energetic, you can have some good walking over these mostly uninhabited hills and the cliffs north of the town.

Puerto de Soller is quite different. It's set in a vast mountain-ringed bay largely lined with yellow sand. And it's a very busy and active port. The road beside the sea has the usual collection of attractive bars and restaurants, and the sandy beach stretches westward from the town's centre, following the curve of the bay. Orange and lemon groves cover much of the surrounding hillslopes. It's a decidedly characterful spot.

Like Puerto de Andraitx, Puerto de Alcudia, and many other small Mallorquín harbours, it came into existence to supply an inland town that served as local market and distribution centre - in this case Soller, spread out on flattish land inside a ring of fantastically jagged mountain peaks four to five miles inland. The climb to Soller is quite steep, and you reach it most easily by a wonderful little tram that adds considerably to Puerto de Soller's characterfulness. And that

impression is further reinforced by the fact that Soller is the terminus of the magnificent little railway that connects the town with Palma. But more about the railway later.

Most of Puerto de Soller's hotels naturally lie a little way from the town centre and sometimes from the beach as well. The sand isn't specially wide, but the view of the town, the harbour, the lovely bay, and the mountains, together with the fact that most people in sight are working and not lounging around with nothing to do, gives the place a decidedly distinctive appeal.

The west coast

Puerto de Soller lies in roughly the middle of the island's west coast and is the only sizable settlement on it. It could almost be described too as the west coast's only true link with the 'real' Majorca. For the fact is that this western side of the island has a fairy-like quality that sets it apart, not only from the rest of Majorca but even from the rest of the world. If you drive the whole of it in a single day - a tough assignment, but just manageable - you'll feel that you came down to earth only at Puerto de Soller.

Describing the drive isn't easy. Even photographs, however skilful, can't fully convey the emotions the west coast stirs. Your sense of sheer wonderment begins when you're past Andraitx, which perches on a steep mountainside a few hundred feet up above Puerto de Andraitx. Despite its fine site the town of Andraitx is itself nothing to write home about.

On the road beyond it, however, climbing towards the thousand-foot Sa Gremola pass on a road with lovely views, your exhilaration begins. It grows when you reach the sea above Punta Jova and you begin to see the whole vast mountain range, with its peaks mostly topping three thousand feet and Puig Mayor reaching almost half as much again, stretching endlessly away to the northeast, while its slopes race straight down to the sea. And all the while you're suspended on a narrow ribbon of road hundreds of feet above the water, often forced inland by the terrain, sometimes having peaks maybe fifteen hundred feet high between you and the water, and every now and again becoming aware of very tiny settlements by the water's edge, at the foot of these overpowering slopes.

Occasionally, on your way north towards Soller and Puerto de Soller, some thirty miles off, you find tiny settlements stretched along the road itself. Only three are of any note.

The first you come to is tiny **Estallencs** (or Estallench in Catalan). It consists of a few lovely old stone houses squeezed in beside road and mountain, one of which offers accommodation that is usually booked out months ahead. Apart from going for walks along the tortuous road and enjoying the breathtaking views there's nothing you can do at Estallencs except take the extremely steep track down to a tiny beach - and of course climb back up at the end of the day. Or make occasional car or scooter excursions.

Another five miles of endless sharp bends and magnificent views bring

you to **Banyalbufar** (or Bañalbufar), an almost ethereal spot. It consists of lots of prosperous-looking, very well kept three- and four-storeyed stone houses, dating from heaven knows when and terraced up the hillsides like the fields they're set amongst. Down by the shore, reached by a road that looks near-vertical, is a tiny beach. The main road's dominant point is a solid-looking little church with a school beside it. The whole place seems unbelievably quiet and peaceful. To crown everything, everyone you meet seems brimful of friendliness.

Should you ever think of returning to Banyalbufar to stay, there are three modest *hostales* (guesthouses) that will put you up.

A further ten miles of contorted road-ribbon, now running mostly inland, take you to the turning leading to Valldemossa and the Carthusian monastery made world-famous by the unhappy stay there in 1838 of the Polish composer Chopin, suffering from tuberculosis, and his difficult French girlfriend, the writer who called herself Georges Sand, not daring in the moral climate of that period to admit publicly to being a *woman* author. But we must keep our minds on the magnificent west coast and leave Valldemossa for the section on inland Majorca.

The next settlement along this dazzling road, **Deia** (or **Deya**), lies seven miles from the Valldemossa turning. If anything, it's even more striking than Banyalbufar, and its history goes back to prehistoric times. Deia's little houses, quite different from Banyalbufar's, cling to the slopes of a conical hill high

53

above the shoreline, and it's thought to have been a Phoenician settlement. Considerable excavation work has been done in recent years. Its more recent development has obviously been very different from Banyalbufar's.

The view from the hilltop is spectacular in the extreme, and way below the little town, reached by a very steep and very narrow road, you come to a tiny beach used by very few people even in the height of the summer season. There's a small hotel just south of Deia, and down - a long way down - on the shore below it you can visit the former home for 53 years of the Austrian Archduke Ludwig Salvator (1847-1915), who spent most of his time on the island compiling the most detailed study ever made of the Balearics archipelago. The English author Robert Graves lived for many years in Deia till his death in 1986.

Another six miles of very tortuous road bring you to the junction with the direct Puerto de Soller-Palma road and the start of the most spectacular part of your journey up Majorca's west coast. Puerto de Soller lies to your left, and Soller, a busy, confusing and not particularly impressive town (apart from its magnificent setting) to your right. Happily you've no need to try to explore Soller. You turn left and after about half a mile right. The road is clearly signposted.

You're coming now into the highest part of the whole west coast range, and peaks topping three thousand feet tower all round you, with the majestic Puig Major straight ahead - well, that's where it would be if the

road were ever straight. But you're twisting and turning all the time, especially as you approach Puig Major and the three thousand foot tunnelled pass below its summit. Unfortunately, some of the huge mountain's impact is removed by the satellite tracking station now very obvious on its summit. All the land even on its flanks has been taken over by the military, and there are notices everywhere warning you off. There's another tunnel on this road further on.

From Soller on the road has been forced well inland, and you're no longer even conscious of the sea - only of the magnificent mountains. After some seventeen miles of them you reach the turning running down to the sea at **Sa Calobra**. This road's very difficult to describe. Of all Europe's so-called scenic routes nothing quite equals this. It resembles a tortured snake slithering down to the sea in a gaunt Mediterranean rock-and-scrub landscape. At one point, a little modestly called 'La Corbata' ('The Tie'), thanks to a tunnel it even twists through a complete 360°. Sa Calobra itself is just a very tiny settlement on the edge of a large, rocky bay. But it has a beach and places you can stay at.

Back again on the road to Cape Formentor another six miles brings you to the Monasterio de Lluc (Lluc Monastery), one of the places to which excursions are offered in summer. Thirteen more mostly winding miles bring you to Pollença, the inland town originally served by Puerto Pollença, which we've already considered. By now you're running downhill and the road has become much easier. **Pollença** itself is a fine old town, whose present streets seem to have been laid out in mediæval times, though its history goes back a great deal further. It possesses the remains of a Roman bridge to its west and a church built by the Knights Templar to the east. The road runs gently down to Puerto de Pollença.

A left turning a little past the town takes you to remote **Cala San Vicente**, a somewhat larger resort than Sa Calobra, but wonderfully shut away in its own colourful rocky bay, with a little sandy beach lying among the rocks.

If you're continuing northward, some of the toughest driving still lies ahead - only ten or eleven miles, it's true, but very hard going. This takes you first up an exhausting series of hairpin bends over the flank of the mountain at the base of the Cabo Formentor peninsula, then on to flatter, heavily wooded ground near its southern coast and the entrance to the Hotel Formentor's superb private estate.

The luxurious and magnificently furnished **Hotel Formentor**, standing in its own vast grounds and lovely garden, with a beach just beyond, is possibly the quietest spot on the whole island. It belongs however to a different age, and the number of people who appreciate its attractions - service, comfort, seclusion and quiet - seems to be more limited. But it's a very lovely spot, with a wonderful view across the Bahia de Pollença to the mountains south of Pollença and the headland on which fortified Alcudia stands.

But there's another eight miles to do battle with before you reach Cabo Formentor's incredible tip and stand beside the lighthouse over six hundred feet above the cliffs dropping vertically into the sea. The lighthouse's beam is visible for nearly forty miles.

When you turn for home your obvious ploy is to swing inland at either Pollença or Puerto de Pollença and take the easy inland road to Palma and your home base. Driving the whole of the west coast in a single day isn't the sort of thing anyone does for relaxation. You can split it up however by covering Palma-Andraitx-Puerto de Soller and back to Palma (or wherever you're staying) on one day, and Palma-Soller-Cape Formentor-Inca-Palma on another. If that seems too much you can split up the second day by turning inland for Selva and Inca just before you reach Lluc Monastery, leaving Cape Formentor for a final excursion. The Firestone map is excellent and signposting in the Majorca countryside is perfectly clear.

Some inland spots

We've seen some glimpses of tiny corners of inland Majorca. What else is there to see and to say? As is true of almost everything in Majorca, quite a lot.

If you drive into the countryside inland from, say, El Arenal, the land looks largely flat, with a few small hills in places and mountains in the distance. The number of windmills pumping up water for irrigation is also very noticeable. This isn't an unfair impression of Majorca's largely level central area.

One or two of the little inland towns attract a proportion of visitors. **Inca's** weekly market has excursions run to it. **Manacor's** artifical pearl factory receives lots of visitors, mostly on their way to the Cuevas del Drach (the Dragon's Caves), just south of Porto Cristo on the eastern coast. The towns themselves however aren't specially exciting. Their main feature is their large churches, many of which look as though they were built as much for defence against marauders as for the worship of God. Not all the settlements are purely agricultural, though. Inca, for instance, is noted for its shoe manufacture.

Petrá is notable for the remarkable Fray Junipero (Brother Juniper), whose birthplace and last resting-place it is. Junipero Serra was born in 1713 and became a Franciscan monk. He went to America when well over fifty. In the wilds of the then untamed western territories he founded almost singlehanded a whole chain of missionary stations - twenty-three of them, stretching over 550 miles and linked by a track he called the Royal Highway, which is well worth travelling today. For us the names of many of his settlements are today household words the whole world round. They include San Diego, Nuestra Señora de los Angeles (Our Lady of the Angels - Los Angeles' original name), Santa Barbara, Santa Cruz, and San Francisco. He must have been quite a man.

Looking at the memorial tablet erected to him on the 250th anniversary of his birth by the people of California and others you can't help wondering what Petrá was like when he grew up there,

and what made him tick strongly enough to achieve such incredible results - and then come back to die in his native town. Petrá's a pleasant spot today, with the usual large church standing on a slight slope offering good views. It obviously meant a lot to Fray Junipero.

The **Cuevas del Drach** (Dragon's Caves) have been mentioned. They provide a very popular day out, with a chance to see a good deal of the island on the way if you're staying anywhere but close to them on the east coast.

It was the redoubtable Archduke Ludwig Salvator (called Luis Salvator in Spanish), living in Son Marroig below Deia, who financed an expedition to explore them, and it was the French speleologist Edouard Martel who discovered their main attraction, an underground lake said to be the world's largest. The caves are well exploited commercially today, with seating for 800 above the lake and a show involving boats and music put on at conveniently regular times. Two of the four caves can be visited. There are other caves on the island, notably those of **Artá** near Playa de Canyamel and **Hams** close to the Cuevas del Drach.

The Carthusian monastery at **Valldemossa** and its connection with Chopin and Georges Sand have also been mentioned. A lot of guidebooks talk about it as a rather miserable place, obviously taking their cue from the unhappy Georges Sand's complaints about the time she spent there with Chopin and showing that their authors can hardly have seen the monastery for themselves. It is in fact charming, with a particularly satisfying view from the rooms which the couple occupied.

Most of the monastery is today a museum devoted largely to Chopin, well worth a visit if you've the least interest in the composer's works. You can see the pianos he used, sketches made at the time of his visit, autographs of compositions, and so on.

Most guidebooks talk about the 'cells' the couple occupied. These are in fact pleasant suites of small rooms, each with its own little formal garden. We know that one of Chopin's Mallorquín friends used to visit him at Valldemossa and play local ballads on his fiddle. What was the music like? Among the traditional instruments preserved in the small museum there's a tiny panpipe. Was that once played regularly in Majorca? A lot of ethnomusicologists would very much like to know. Too much of Spain's traditional folk music has vanished, alas.

One of the Spanish books in the library consists of an impassioned plea for the encouragement of tourism in Majorca. It was published in 1906.

Most tour operators and many local firms offer a pretty wide range of excursions on Majorca, including a number by boat to places like the island of **Cabrera**, some twenty miles outside Palma's bay, or to nearer resorts. One trip however you ought to make by yourself - a simple train ride from Palma to either Soller or Inca. If you go to Soller you can continue by the famous local tram to Puerto de

Soller. Or of course if you're staying in Puerto de Soller you can make this your means of visiting Palma. Rumbling gently across country in the little open-sided two-coach train, enjoying the landscapes with nothing to obstruct your view, and dropping finally into the ring of massive, jagged peaks surrounding Soller is a very pleasant experience - and one that tens of thousands of visitors enjoy every summer.

If you hire a car or scooter you can wander about the island in a very leisurely way. You can go to **Randa**, for instance, 25 miles east of Palma, and climb to the hilltop monastery of Nuestra Señora de Cura for the view over Majorca's central plain to the mountains beyond. Or spend a pleasant time in the lovely **Alfabia** gardens on the road between Palma and Soller. They were part of a large Moorish estate in the fourteenth century.

Palma de Mallorca

It remains to say a few words about Majorca's (and the Balearics') magnificent capital, **Palma**. The first time you see the town you'll wonder why such relatively poor islands (as they once were) have such a beautifully built and prosperous-looking capital. The answer quite simply is that for many centuries, as long as all the places round the Mediterranean traded mainly with each other and sent their cargoes by sea, the Catalans held a leading place in this carrying trade. And Palma was a major Catalan trading base. Transport patterns have changed today. Each Mediterranean island, in particular, is almost totally tied to the mainland country that's its political parent. And the mainland holds the purse strings.

Palma's vast bay is superb, and the backdrop of hills and mountains is impressive. A magnificent dual-carriageway road lined with palms, called the Paseo Maritimo, sweeps round the city's seafront, providing a fast through route. And, dominating everything, the massive and imposing Cathedral seems to be keeping a wary and watchful eye on everything that's going on.

If you look at any good town plan of Palma - the Firestone T26, with a Palma street plan on its reverse side is excellent - you'll see a star-shaped ring of broad avenues surrounding a tangle of narrow alleys. This is the town's old centre. The avenues follow the line of the now vanished seventeenth century fortifications. Remains of even earlier walls can be seen just east of the Cathedral, above the infill of flat land used to extend the shoreline into deeper water as the size of cargo vessels increased.

You reach the Cathedral up some steps, with the harbour master's office, now some way from the shore, on your left. The Cathedral stands on the site of a former mosque. Its building began soon after 1235 and was spread over 400 years. Most of what you see today dates from the fourteenth and fifteenth centuries, and very impressive it is. The Cathedral's west front, containing the main entrance, and the huge, soaring nave can only be described as majestic. When the sun's shining - as it usually is for much of the year - the blaze of colour from the stained

glass windows is almost dazzling.

The large building immediately west of the Cathedral, known as the Almudaina Palace, was originally a Moorish fort. In the fourteenth and fifteenth centuries it was converted into a royal Catalan palace. Today it houses government offices.

You reach the very attractive Plaza Mayor (Main Square) up the street between the Almudaina and the Cathedral. Just keep going as straight as you can. On your way there, in the Calle Almudaina, you'll see some fine seventeenth and eighteenth century noblemen's houses. And if you want to enjoy more of the narow old streets and their buildings try branching off to your right from the Plaza Cort (which you pass through on your way to the Plaza Mayor) and making a little circular tour. Palma's fine seventeenth century Town Hall stands in the Plaza Cort. But the whole of this old part of the town is attractive to stroll through, and usually fairly cool in the heat of even a summer afternoon.

Some newer building inside the old town is attractive too. A few yards west of the Plaza Mayor the long, straight, wide Via Roma contains excellent shops. It's usually referred to as just La Rambla (the Avenue). Another good shopping street is the impressive Paseo dés Borne, to give it its official (Catalan) title. It's usually called just El Borne (in Spanish). It used to be known as the Paseo Generalísimo Franco, a name still sometimes used.

You'll no doubt do your own wandering around Palma and, if you're staying near the capital, find your own favourite shops, bars, and nightspots. Everyone does. But there are a couple more very distinctive buildings on the old town's seafront that you ought to have a look at. Flanked by impressive tall palms, they stand a little west of the Almudaina. One is the five hundred year old Lonja, or Exchange, where merchants once met to do business. Its architect, a local man called Guillermo Sagrera (the street outside is named after him) built also Perpignan's fine Cathedral and the great hall of Alfonso V's Castel Nuovo in Naples. The Lonja's towers and turrets and gargoyles may make you think it's a church. But it isn't and never was. Today it houses Majorca's Museum of Fine Arts.

The building immediately west of the Lonja is the seventeenth century Consulado del Mar, Palma's equivalent of Perpignan's Loge de Mer. It was originally used as a law court where cases involving commercial or maritime disputes were settled. It's a naval museum today.

High above the town the great castle of Bellver (Catalan for the French Bellevue) justifies its name completely. The view over Palma Bay is superb, and the nearby Son Vida eighteen-hole golf course has a very good reputation. Down in the town another Pueblo Español, copied from Barcelona's, displays various types of traditional Spanish houses. It's unfortunately rather tame and unexciting, especially after Barcelona's.

Palma can be treated as basically an excursion centre, which is what it will be for most visitors to Majorca. It does however have a number of good modern hotels overlooking the sea towards its western side. They've no beach within easy reach. But several have swimming pools, and some have terraces where you can get plenty of sun during the day and enjoy a magnificent view over Palma and its harbour when the sun has gone down. They're especially pleasant to stay at outside the main summer season.

MENORCA

As its name implies, Menorca (often spelled Minorca in English) is the 'lesser' or 'smaller' island compared with 'greater' Majorca. It measures little more than thirty miles by twelve. The land is mostly rolling plateau, with the highest point 1148 feet above sea level. That's Monte Toro in the island's centre, one of only six hills of noticeable eminence. Its nearest rival is a good 250 feet lower.

Gaunt cliffs, not specially high, line the northern shore, broken by only a few inlets containing resorts or villages. Good beaches, backed by woods and rocky shorelines that are rather less wild than most of Majorca's, are found on the other coasts. Mahon and Ciudadela, on oposite sides of Menorca, are two colourful but contrasting towns. The first is the present capital and administrative and communications centre, the second an ancient citadel and fortress town.

Relics of far more ancient settlements are scattered over almost all Menorca's landscapes in the shape of the strange prehistoric *talayots* and *navetas*. The former are large conical stone mounds,

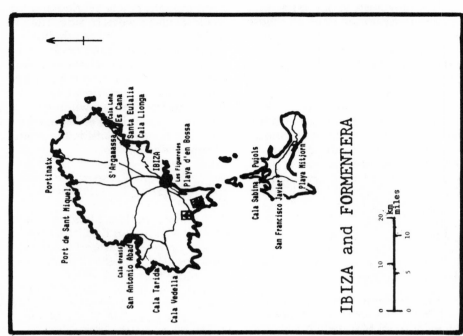

IBIZA and FORMENTERA

Portinatx

Port de Sant Miquel

Cala Grasió
San Antonio Abad

Cala Tarida

Cala Vedella

S'Arganassa
Cala Leña
Es Cana
Santa Eulalia
Cala Llonga

IBIZA

Les Figueretas
Playa d'en Bossa

Cala Sabina Pujols

San Francisco Javier

Playa Mitjorn

km
miles

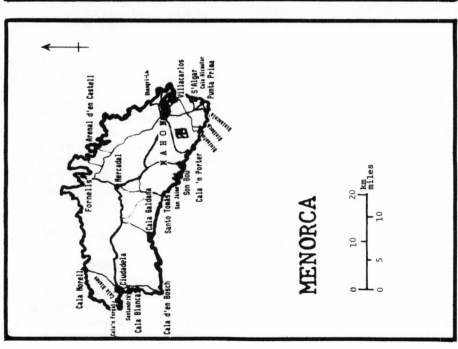

MENORCA

Cala Morell

Cala'n Forcat
Santandria
Cala Blanca

Ciudadela

Cala d'en Bosch

Fornells

Mercadal

Cala Galdana

Santo Tomás
San Jaime
Son Bou
Cala 'n Porter

Arenal d'en Castell

Shangri-La

MAHON

Villacarlos
S'Algar
Cala Alcaufar
Punta Prima

Binibeca
Binisafua

km
miles

topped by fortified dwellings and grouped together to make up little settlements, some of them protected by what appear to have been town walls. The **navetas** are remarkable and unique stone structures, found nowhere else, whether in the Mediterranean or elsewhere. They are shaped like upturned boats. No one has yet identified their function with any convincing certainty. But they could well be burial chambers.

A remarkable number of villas and holiday flats have been built on Menorca, along with a rather more restricted proportion of modern hotels. In its scenery the island lacks totally the extraordinary and striking contrasts that Majorca provides. The high winds that occasionally sweep across it meet no obstructions similar to Majorca's mountains. They put a premium on sheltered positions for the island's holiday resorts. Yet many people consider Menorca the ideal place for holidays, especially for those with young families or those who want a really peaceful time. That doesn't by any means mean that there's no entertainment and nothing to do in the evenings. Far from it. But the island's main characteristic is certainly peace.

Menorca's resorts

If you come by air you land at Menorca airport, only 2½ miles from the capital, Mahon. The town stands at the inner end of a long, deep, east-facing narrow bay which was a major base for the English Mediterranean fleet from 1708 to 1783. Directly south of Mahon, round the island's southeastern

extremity, a number of self-catering settlements have been constructed since the war. Some have been grafted onto older hamlets. But in character and atmosphere they're entirely modern. All consist of white painted villas or small blocks of flats in what is generally considered 'Mediterranean' style, a variation of what in France is (wrongly) called 'Provençal'. All they really have in common with any sort of traditional Mediterranean domestic building is the white paint. But that doesn't mean they're unattractive.

Cala'n Porter (or **Ca'n Porter**), roughly ten miles southwest of Mahon, consists of scores and scores of small white, red-roofed villas neatly spread out in a boulder-and-scrub landscape. The road to a smallish, but a deep beach of firm sand flanked by medium-height cliffs, runs down one side of the settlement. There are bars on the beach's edge, with houses and flats above. At the season's end, the wind is quite capable of penetrating to this beach despite its sheltering cliffs.

Binisafua and adjoining **Binibeca**, reached by a turning off the Cala'n Porter-Mahon road halfway from Mahon, are rather similar, except that Binisafua has a decidedly Moorish tinge to its architecture (its name's Moorish, anyway). Binibeca is plainer. Their beaches are a good deal smaller than Cala'n Porter's.

Punta Prima on the island's tip, **Biniancola** immediately west, and **S'Algar** on its east-facing coast are plain, simple modern holiday settlements, consisting mainly of self-catering establishments, though with modern hotel accommodation at S'Algar. **Cala Alcaufar** itself has one hotel poised above its beach and other accommodation rather further inland. It's a typically tiny Menorcan seaside settlement, with tourist accommodation built around a tiny original village.

From S'Algar you can make the half-mile walk to the little beach at Cala Alcaufar to swim or sunbathe - unless you prefer the saltwater pool across the road or the rocks on the nearby shore. As in much of Menorca, the S'Algar hotel provides its own evening entertainment.

There are other rather similar holiday settlements in the further side of the island's capital, Mahon, including one called **Shangri-La**.

West of Cala'n Porter three delightful small resorts and a wonderful mile-long sandy beach, as yet relatively undeveloped, occupy the centre of the island's south coast. The vast **Son Bou** beach is the most easterly. Till recently it was known only to archaeologists because of the remains of a very early Christian church nearby. The beach is backed by a quite steep slope. Today both Son Bou itself and the village of **San Jaime**, which shares its beach, are growing into attractive holiday spots.

If you're driving you've a good fifteen miles of very attractive hilly and wooded inland road to reach the next resort, **Santo Tomás**. On foot it's only a few minutes across a low headland - but from the mile-long Son Bou-San Jaime beach's western end. There's another long beach here, with villas and a few shops set back a little way from it.

The land round about is largely flat.

Getting to our fourth resort, **Cala Galdana**, barely four miles off along the coast, involves yet another fiften miles of driving on more of Menorca's quiet roads through rolling woodland and open fields. This is a quite wonderful and wonderfully secluded spot. Its long sandy beach stretches away eastward from a long, narrow creek filled with colourful yachts. Of the two main hotels, one stands directly above the beach, and the other west of the creek and a little inland. There's little sign of the 'commercialisation' - rows of souvenir kiosks and the like - normal in so many recently-built resorts. This seems to be another of Menorca's special features, noticeable not only at Cala Galdana.

The back of the resort's curving beach merges into a sandy area well shaded by maritime pines. It also shelves very gently, making the spot ideal for young children. Since it's reached by a dead-end approach and has no road backing the beach you could hardly find a safer spot. And there aren't many small resorts anywhere that are more beautiful.

The last south coast resort, **Cala d'en Bosch** (or **Ca'n Bosch** or even plain **Playa Bosch**) is even more deliberately designed for safety. To reach it you have to park your car and approach by a footbridge that crosses a narrow channel leading to a little circular harbour. Again, it's an extremely simple and an extremely colourful spot, surrounded by shady pines sloping down to a not specially large beach.

A rather more extensive development, consisting mostly of villas and called **Tamarinda**, lies immediately west of Cala d'en Bosch.

We're now at the island's southwestern extremity, with Ciudadela about six miles to the north. The first half of the road runs a little inland, and then closer to the sea. There are no real resorts here - only a good deal of rather straggling tourist development. Some of it is nondescript but some, including **Cala Blanca**, is quite attractive. **Santandria**, in particular, close to the lighthouse, is worth noticing, though its beach isn't very large.

Ciudadela itself is a delightfully unpretentious small town of white- or colour-washed houses and cool patios set in narrow streets. Its harbour was large enough to be used by the biggest seagoing vessels before the days of steam, and for centuries it was the island's main defence against corsair raids. Its name in fact means Citadel.

A lofty memorial in the town's main square, the Plaza del Borne, commemorates a particularly spirited defence of the town against a Moslem raid in 1588. You'll find some beautiful old mansions with loggias and colourful patios in the streets around the square. The Moorish Alcázar (fort) is now a small museum. Its exhibits include the banner carried by King Alfonso III of Catalonia and Aragón when he recaptured Menorca in 1287, and a picture of King George III of England left over from the days when we ruled the island. The Cathedral dates from 1370, the seventeenth century church of San

Agustín contains some fine frescos, and the thirteenth century San Francisco's side chapels possess elegant altarpieces.

A further line of of modern developments stretches around the broad headland west of Ciudadela. They include yet another quiet little cove, **Cala'n Forçat**, lined with rocks and with a very gently sloping small sandy beach. It's not a resort in itself, but there are enough bars, restaurants, and shops within walking distance to cope with most of your needs. **Cala Blanes** nearby offers self-catering accommodation.

On your way out of Ciudadela - the main road runs eastward and you've not a lot of choice - it's worth pausing for a few moments to inspect the **Naveta d'es Tudons**, one of the best-preserved of these unexplained prehistoric buildings. It's solidly constructed of plain stones, and shaped very like an upturned ship's hull about 46 feet long. There's an entrance big enough to crawl through at one end, but nothing special to see inside. If you want to see the *talayots*, they're dotted about all over the island and are marked on the Firestone T26. There's one with a specially good 'altar' among the other buildings - or whatever the flat-topped structure was - at **Trepuco** between Mahon and San Luis to its south.

The north coast's only main resort, **Arenal d'en Castell**, stands above a small sandy beach set inside a large, well-sheltered bay. The beach slopes very gently and is bounded by rocks. It's ideal for small children - and also for watersports. The wooded surroundings are charming, and the resort has a scattering of bars, shops, and restaurants, but not much else.

West of Arenal d'en Castell, with the usual long inland drive to reach it, there's a nine-hole golf course, the **Son Parc**, where you can also spend holidays. There's a small beach resort close to it and, set towards the tip of a large, very well-sheltered bay, the attractive small fishing village of **Fornells**. Its bars and restaurants specialise in fish meals and are worth visiting, but Fornells isn't a major resort. It is however a very pleasant village, set in a wonderfully picturesque rocky bay and reached by a notably pleasant road.

Both Fornells and Arenal d'en Castell are linked to the capital, Mahon, by an extremely attractive and quiet road which avoids the busy main thoroughfare between Ciudadela and Mahon. Nearly all Menorca's commercial vehicles seem to be constantly on the move between these two towns. If you want to explore the island it's well worth hiring a car for two or three days at least, so as to take in some of the very quiet minor roads and remoter corners.

The only other north coast resort is **Cala Morell**, reached by a five-mile side road from Ciudadela. Its accommodation is nearly all self-catering.

The island's capital, **Mahon**, occupies a lovely position deep on the southern side of the magnificent east coast bay which has served as an important anchorage since Phoenician days, but mainly for fighting ships rather than for commerce. Much of the present-day town has been built in recent times, including a number of tourist hotels. The older part is grouped around the Plaza de España, linked to the harbour by a flight of steps. The Town Hall in the Plaza del Generalísimo Franco dates from the seventeenth century and is one of the town's few notable buildings. The former farmhouse where Nelson and Lady Hamilton lived for a time in 1799 stands on the bay's northern side and is now a museum.

Villacarlos, adjacent to Mahon on the bay's southern side, is a very peaceful and likeable little town, perched above a long, curving quayside. From here you look across to massive naval barracks dating from the years of British occupation. And, curiously enough, there still seem to be a tremendous number of local people around who speak good English. Have old habits really lasted that long?

Finally, note that the quiet inland towns of **San Luis**, just south of the airport, and **Mercadal**, very centrally placed below Monte Torro, are becoming popular with visitors. Car hire's cheap, the island's small, and with these places as bases you can choose your beach or outing to suit each day's mood.

IBIZA

If Ibiza had to be described in a single word, that word would be 'miniature'. It isn't a lot smaller in area than Menorca, but the curious thing about it is that everything seems to have been scaled down. There are even miniature mountain passes when you drive to Portinatx in the north and when you cross the

Tiny Cala 'n Forçat is typical of many of Menorca's peaceful coastal spots.

Marbella's well-known Puerto José Banus marina sets
enviable standards of luxury.

Pick your Own - outside the Lonja building on Palma de Mallorca's seafront.

Granada's magnificent Moorish palace, the Alhambra,
occupies a superb position at the foot of the Sierra
Nevada (the Snowy Mountain).

island between the two main settlements of Ibiza town, the capital, and San Antonio Abad. Only the very pleasant capital seems full-sized apart perhaps from the bustling modern resort that has grown up around San Antonio Abad's large open bay. And even so, the little fortified old Upper Town (Dalt Vila) climbing up the hill beside modern Ibiza town feels almost like a toy.

Ibiza island's only other notable features are its many white-painted little cube-shaped cottages, similar to those you see in Puglia, the region of Italy's 'heel', and its fortified churches, designed as refuges against attack by sea-borne raiders.

For modern visitors, driving over miniature mountains (the highest point is barely 1500 feet above the sea) and through tiny white-painted villages, the fortified churches (eg, at San Miguel and above Santa Eulalia) provide a picturesque reminder of days past. The cube homes of Italy are direct descendants of Puglia's primitive stone *trulli*, themselves closely related to the primitive one-roomed huts in which many of our remote ancestors lived. The same may be true of Ibiza's. For all their elemental shape and tiny size, however, Ibiza island's little cottages are perfectly comfortable and extremely pleasant to look at.

The island's layout is easily described. Ibiza town lies in the southern part of the east coast, with San Antonio Abad opposite it on the west coast. One main resort lies on flat land south of Ibiza town, and a little string of them further north.

San Antonio's large bay is nearly full of modern hotels, and new resorts are growing up to its south. More new resorts are being built on small bays in the north, and there's a well-established self-catering settlement on high ground between San Antonio and Ibiza town.

Ibiza's resorts

San Antonio Abad (St Anthony the Abbot - to distinguish him from other St Anthonys) is far and away the island's biggest and liveliest resort. The original tiny, white-painted town, was once a very peaceful spot. It lies on the large bay's northern side, with one or two modern hotels and a rather small beach directly south of it. Today it has become the very lively centre of a resort whose hotels are scattered all round the bay. In the little town itself you'll find plenty of discos, bars, restaurants, and English-style pubs. The majority of the hotels however are a little way away, scattered round the large bay's shore, which is lined with a mixture of crags and sandy beaches. In some cases buses run into San Antonio from the hotels. In others it's easier to take one of the frequent ferries assuming, that is, that you feel the need to go into town.

Most people will want to have a look at it, and you'll have to go there if you want to travel into Ibiza town on your own and not on an excursion bus - unless you hire a car or scooter, of course. But there's usually at least a sprinkling of shops and bars around your hotel and enough evening entertainment to keep most people happy. The town itself has achieved a tremendous reputation as a lively centre for younger folk. That doesn't mean the whole bay area is inadvisable for families - just that you may think it worthwhile to ask your travel agent exactly where the hotel you fancy is located, what it's like, and what sort of entertainment, shops, bars, and so on you'll find close to it.

There's a small resort area to San Antonio's north, little more than a mile from the centre, at **Cala Grasió**. It's virtually a suburb of the town. As elsewhere round the bay, rocks and crags form the shoreline, interspersed with sandy bays and backed by pinewoods.

About six miles to the south, a modern resort is growing at tiny **Cala Tarida**, where there's a small but pleasant sandy beach flanked by the usual rocks and crags. This, in 1987, is still more or less virgin territory, providing all its own activities. Much the same applies to **Cala Vedella**, about four miles south of Cala Tarida, but reached by a long inland detour through the village of San José.

On the island's other side you can choose between six resorts in all. The most southerly, **Playa d'en Bossa**, stands within sight of Ibiza's Old Town and is unusual both because of its level terrain and because of its enormous open beach - some two miles of excellent sand. Further, the settlement is totally modern. It contrives to combine being an extremely lively spot in its built-up area with a feeling of real remoteness at the beach's southern end. It has a good choice of bars and restaurants - including English-style pubs - and a number of discos.

Les Figueretes (Las Figueretas in Spanish) also lies south of the island's capital, with a large pebbly beach and modern hotels. It's more or less a suburb of Ibiza town, with nearness to a good choice of shops, bars, and restaurants one of its attractions.

The four other holiday spots on the island's east coast are all based on tiny older settlements now making a virtually continuous ribbon of mixed development along seven or eight miles of the road nearest the coast (which isn't always very near). The liveliest link in the chain is Santa Eulalia.

Cala Llonga is the one you reach first travelling north from Ibiza town, some ten miles away. It's tucked away at the base of a deep little bay lined with wooded cliffs flanking a good sandy beach.

It's a quiet spot that stretches into the rather livelier **Santa Eulalia**, the east coast's only town apart from Ibiza itself. At least, with all its shops,bars, cafés, and its waterfront promenade (a marina's due soon) it feels like a town compared with the island's tiny villages. What's more, the town has a distinctly Spanish rather than Balearic-Catalan feel to it. Behind the sandy beaches the land's flat enough to allow open views of the inland hills - unusual on Ibiza - and also to make cycle hire worthwhile. This is especially the case if you want to wander along the coast. If you walk you'll find there are footpaths in places leading from one cove to another, but too often you have to make an inland détour. Buses don't help, and anyway aren't frequent enough. The alternative is to use the boats that link this line of resorts.

Tiny **S'Argamassa** links Santa Eulalia to Es Cana. In essence it's a small and very quiet modern development on a headland with small beaches close by. The built-up area at **Es Cana** is rather larger, and the place enjoys a more spacious feel. The beach here is sandy and quite large and its hinterland flat and dotted with pines. These soon give way to fairly intensive cultivation. Es Cana has a harbour, some shops, and a lively weekly hippy market. There are one or two discos, but nightlife here, as in the neighbouring resorts, is hardly anyone's major interest. Beyond Es Cana there's a small holiday club at **Cala Leña** with its own small beach.

There remain two small resorts in the island's northwest. **Portinatx** is a delightful spot, reached from Ibiza town by a twenty-mile drive through scenery of hills and woods and occasional tiny villages that are pleasant all the way. You also cross one of Ibiza's miniature mountain passes. And when you reach Portinatx the road runs steeply down among the pines to dunes and a very attractive wide sandy beach enclosed by wooded headlands. This is very much the end of the road, though there are a few shops and one or two restaurants. It's a fairly obvious choice if you're taking young children with you.

Port de Sant Miquel (or Puerto de San Miguel if you prefer the Spanish, or almost any combination of the words if you know neither language), only four or five miles from Portinatx as the crows fly but nearly thirty miles by road, has been even more recently developed than Portinatx. The resort has grown up around the tiny harbour that served the little inland market town of Sant Miquel in the days when roads were nearly non-existent and sea transport was vastly easier and cheaper. Port de Sant Miquel provides a pleasant beach of sand and rocks and a certain amount of nightlife. Its cliff and woodland setting is attractive.

Excursions on Ibiza

If you're staying in or near Santa Eulalia you'll possibly make the effort to walk up to the fortified church. You'll certainly go into San Antonio town once or twice if you've chosen a hotel near the town. From most resorts an 'island tour' by coach is regularly on offer, which may include a visit to the extensive saltpans just south of the airport (you get a very good view as you arrive). Boat trips to the island of Formentera, described below, taking about an hour each way, are also possible. Wandering around the island by hire car or scooter is decidedly attractive. You'll need the Firestone T26, of course. But the only real excursion destination is Ibiza town.

Ibiza town is a fascinating place. As far as we know it was first settled by Carthaginians based in North Africa but descended from Phoenician (alias Punic) ancestors from Asia Minor. Five hundred years later the Romans conquered it. Another five hundreds years passed before Vandal invaders captured it from the Romans, only to lose it a century later to a Byzantine fleet when the vast Roman empire had split in two and Byzantium (modern Istanbul) ruled its eastern Mediterranean lands and some of the western Med's coasts. Two more centuries passed before Moorish invaders settled there. It was 1235 before Jaime I of Catalonia conquered it and enabled it eventually to become part of modern Spain. A surprising amount of all this history can still be seen in relics on the ground.

The main part of the town - El Pueblo Nuevo or New Town - dates from the nineteenth century and contains pleasant shops, bars, and restaurants. The old fishing area east of it - La Peña (Sa Penya in Catalan) - is also pleasant to stroll through, and the main harbour to the west invariably has something of interest going on. It's the Upper Town however, the very colourful **Dalt Vila**, that is the main attraction.

You enter it up a wide ramp leading to the massive Las Tablas gateway (Portal de las Tablas). The coat of arms over the gate was carved in 1585, thirty years after Philip II of Spain (whom we remember for the Armada) had started giving the Dalt Vila its present massive fortifications, intending to make Ibiza a major naval base.

It doesn't matter which route you take inside the gateway. In a very short time you'll have seen the whole of the Dalt Vila. Be warned however. The going's very steep and you need comfortable shoes for the cobbles.

The main places of interest include the eighteenth century church of Santo Domingo, with a richly-carved interior; the Town Hall (Ayuntamiento), formerly a Dominican monastery dating from the fifteenth century with lovely cloisters attached; a Roman temple rebuilt after near-total destruction in the eighteenth century; the thirteenth century Cathedral built on the site of a Moorish mosque; and the Archaeological Museum alongside the Cathedral, which has an interesting collection of antiquities going back to the Carthaginian, Roman, and Moorish settlements.

Below the Dalt Vila and south of the modern town centre you can visit one of the most notable Carthaginian burial grounds ever discovered. It has hundreds of tombs carved in rock. Many of the fine sarcophagi from them can be seen in the nearby Puig des Molins (Windmill Hill) Museum.

FORMENTERA

An hour or so's journey by ferry from Ibiza town makes you realise how very different the four main Balearic Islands are from each other. Unlike all its neighbours, tiny **Formentera** consists mainly of a broad mosaic of tiny fields punctuated by vast figtrees. The island's barely ten miles long and a mile wide at its narrow 'waist'. Once its only buildings were white-painted farms and windmills. In recent years however small modern resorts have started to grow beside its impressive beaches. The south-facing **Playa Mitjorn**, with its enormous expanse of gleaming sand, is outstanding, and there's another good sandy beach, **Cala**

Sabina, on Formentera's western shore. Quite a lot of visitors have become hooked on these beaches, and return regularly.

Recent development has been slow, with Playa Mitjorn in the lead, though it's still very small. While most hotels provide some sort of evening entertainment, **Pujols** in the north is the main centre for what real nightlife there is. Inland **San**

Francisco Javier, centrally placed on the island's spine, is its working capital. The island's main obstacle to tourist development is the fact that its water supply is apt to be a trifle salty, which can upset some people's digestion. Drink bottled mineral water and avoid too much tea or coffee. The beaches are ideal for toddlers provided you keep an eye on what they drink.

THE ISLANDS' YEAR

5 January The Festival of the Three Kings is specially colourful in Palma, where they cross the bay by boat. Celebrations include fireworks.

16/17 January St Anthony the Abbot's Day is celebrated in Palma, Artá, La Puebla, and of course San Antonio Abad. It's also celebrated at Manacor, where it's mixed with a festival believed to be Moorish in origin.

17 January Ciudadela celebrates a battle between Moors and Christians.

Holy Week (the week leading up to Easter Day) There are specially picturesque celebrations at Palma and Pollença (where a torchlight procession climbs the steps to the Calvary).

8-10 May Soller celebrates a battle between Moors and Christians.

18-24 May Festival of St John, celebrated with great intensity in Ciudadela, with processions, horse-

riding competitions, and so on.

28 June St Peter's Eve in Alcudia. Boat processions, public High Mass, etc.

July Many local celebrations.

30 July-5 August Feast of Our Lady of the Snows in Ibiza town. This includes races for Ibizenco dogs (a special and ancient breed), fireworks, regatta, trotting races, bullfights.

2 August Pollença celebrates yet another battle between Moors and Christians. Festivities include a log-chopping competition.

11 August Festival of Santa Candida at Llucmajor.

7 September Feast of Our Lady of Grace at Mahon. Horse races, concerts, processions, and folk dancing.

24 September Binisalem holds its grape harvest festival. Free wine is dispensed.

6.   The Rest of Spain's Eastern Med Coast

We come now to a part of Spain that's very different from what we've seen so far. The Catalan influence has disappeared, of course. So for the most part have the rocky creeks and cliffs so prominent along the Costa Brava and around the Balearic Islands. For much of the way this is a region of *huertas* (intensely cultivated, carefully irrigated citrus orchards), of olive groves, of rice fields, and of palmgroves, where the mountains only occasionally crash down to the sea (notably at Cabo de la Nao, which has Denia on its northern side and Calpe and Benidorm to the south), where the land inland from the shore is usually flat, and where huge sandy beaches exist that most Brits have still never even heard of. Most were developed for tourism relatively late. Yet they're among Spain's finest. But perhaps the modern practice of building large hotel swimming pools (with bars alongside) is making natural beaches less important.

Access in this region has long been something of a problem for international holidaymakers. This stretch of the coast's length, from the River Ebro to Cabo de Gata, is a good five hundred miles, further even than London to Aberdeen. The main charter airport, Alicante, is centrally placed. It was perhaps inevitable that the resorts close to Alicante - Benidorm, Denia, and the rest - should be the first to become popular. But Valencia and Almeria airports, north and south respectively, are now taking a bigger traffic share. Even so, the majority of their resorts are filled with Spanish rather than international tourists.

Except for Benidorm, even those popular with foreign tourists are mostly fairly quiet. Privately-owned apartments play a major role in the region's tourism.

We ought, for exactness sake, to get the various Costas' names correct. Tour operators - mapmakers too I'm afraid, including Firestone's HQ who ought to know better - are vague about them.

The most northerly section, in the Provinces of Castellón de la Plana and Valencia, is appropriately called the Costa del Azahar (Orange Blossom Coast). It's where most of Spain's vast orange crop is grown. Next comes the Costa Blanca (White Coast), lying wholly in the Province of Alicante. Again, its name is appropriate: the vast stretches of sand really are glaring white. South of that comes the Costa Cálida, the Warm Coast, which is part of Murcia Province, where the climate really is remarkably warm. Finally, the Costa de Almeria, taking its name directly from its province, fills the east-facing coast as far as the Cabo de Gata (Cat's Cape), Spain's southeastern tip, and carries on round the cape to the most westerly section of the country's south-facing coast. As a matter of convenience this chapter ends halfway through the Costa de Almeria, at the Cabo de Gata.

Resorts of the Costa del Azahar

The first settlement we come to after crossing the provincial boundary beyond the River Ebro's vast estuary (described in the chapter on the Costa Brava and Costa Dorada) is Vinaroz. It's simply a large fishing port. The next, Benicarló is similar but smaller. From here a road close to the coast takes you the five miles to **Peñiscola**, whose central fortified old town - the walls date from the late sixteenth century - is perched on a rocky peninsular with large sandy beaches on either side. The town's only access road (from Benicarló) flanks the northerly beach.

If you ever visit Peñiscola you'll find that everyone expects you to be familiar with the story of the Aragonese Cardinal Pedro de Luna. Elected Pope in 1394 as Benedict XIII (or, rather, 'antipope', to use the historians' term), during the Great Schism when the Western world had two rival popes, he never got anywhere near the Vatican. Instead he retreated to Peñiscola, lived happily till past eighty, and named his successor before he died. You can see his coat of arms on one of the castle gates above the modern town. The castle and the old town make attractive outings. Peñiscola itself is a charmingly quiet spot.

South of it cliffs and mountain foothills drive road and railway inland for a whole forty miles. There are however a number of sandy beaches in a very shallow bay around the town of **Alcocéber**, reached by a three-mile turning off the main road. This is one of the region's many up-and-coming resorts.

The road returns to the sea at **Oropesa de Mar**, another old town perched on a headland, this time with a vast curving beach south of it and a modern resort, popular with Spanish holidaymakers and containing a lot of self-catering villas and flats, developing alongside. Another stretch of cliffs separates Oropesa from the resort usually called **Benicasim**, though its name is strictly Las Villas de Benicasim. The original Benicasim is the town just inland. Here there's another excellent long beach and a number of hotels and apartment blocks, backed by a long rolling hill-slope covered with orange groves. Self-catering holidays are also available here.

Beaches and intermittent modern tourist developments continue along the coast for over ten miles. The Playa de las Villas, as Benicasim's beach is called, is separated from the neighbouring Playa del Pinar and the resort town of **El Grao** only by a low headland. El Grao is partly a fishing and commercial port, but mostly nowadays the weekend playground of people from the provincial capital **Castellón de la Plana**, some three miles inland. El Grao can boast a really enormous beach. Castellón itself stands in the middle of a vast, completely flat *huerta*.

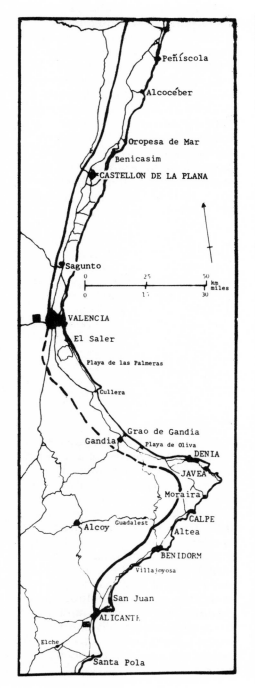

There's nothing further of special interest till you reach the town of **Sagunto**, lying on a small estuary about three miles inland. It's a place of tremendous historical importance, with a lot of fascinating archaeological remains - notably the citadel and the fortifications, houses, temples and so on built not only by the Iberian tribesmen who inhabited the place before even the Carthaginians arrived, but also by the Carthaginians, and later the Romans, Visigoths, Arabs and - one feels - virtually everyone else. Unfortunately it's also the site of a huge steelworks, for which its harbour imports coal while exporting a lot of the local oranges. It's not a particularly attractive spot.

At Sagunto you've already crossed into Valencia Province, and you're only twelve miles or so from Valencia itself. Valencia has a sizable sort of town beach to its north. Its harbour, like Castellón's, is called El Grao. On the city's southern side there's a long series of sandy beaches. The biggest and, so far, most developed is **El Saler**, with an early *parador* and a well-known golf course right on the beach. **Playa de Las Palmeras** is also quite a sizable resort. The whole inland area is filled with ricefields and, in its northern part, by the freshwater La Albufera lagoon.

A small rocky headland and the little harbour of **Cullera** at the mouth of the River Júcar separate this string of beaches from yet another long line of them to the south. Again, a sizable resort is growing up south of Cullera. But it's of interest mainly to Spaniards. While the main road takes an inland route, following the line of the older track on higher ground, the beaches continue along the coast. Some, notably **Grao de Gandia** (also called just Gandia, though that's strictly just the inland town), are backed by considerable tourist building. But none seems to attract much attention from foreign tour operators. Just beyond **Playa de Oliva**, which has several sandy beaches on its northern side, we reach the boundary of Valencia Province and the end of the Costa del Azahar.

Resorts of the Costa Blanca

Denia is an old port settlement whose extensive modern villa-and-flat development has made it home from home for many Scandinavians and Germans, as well as large numbers of Brits, both expatriates and holidaymakers. It lies on a peaceful stretch of coast, reached by a turning off the main Valencia-Alicante road, in a setting of orange groves, palms, and tall yew hedges. Good sandy beaches can be found on either side of the town, and pleasant walks over the cliffs are possible. There's no shortage of British pubs and other entertainment here, and the shops are excellent. Because of the vast amount of residential accommodation, restaurants have a rather casual atmosphere. Denia is very much a family settlement. The weekly market, the harbour, and the old town, reached by a ten or fifteen-minute bus ride from the main resort area, all provide pleasant alternatives to lying on the beach. Car excursions into the inland mountains are pleasant and easy.

Denia is the first town forming part of a broad headland of rocks and cliffs that is part of the Sierra de Alfaro range, which comes straight down to the sea around Cabo de la Nao. A narrow and winding, but direct, road takes you into Jávea. The main road has meanwhile abandoned the coast completely and runs a considerable way inland on a route that includes a gorge at one point and the narrow high street, lined with souvenir shops, of **Gata de Gorgos** at another. Gata de Gorgos is a colourful little spot.

Jávea possesses another of the Costa Blanca's great sandy beaches, in addition to a specially-built *parador* dating from the days when the Spanish government was still trying to attract visitors to Spain's less well known areas. It's also a major yachting centre, with a first-rate harbour tucked away under a sheltering headland at the beach's northern end, as well as a pretty lively resort. The cliffs of the Cabo de la Nao stare out to sea some five miles south of the last bit of Jávea's beach. They've some minor tourist development around them, but the mountains inland are nearly roadless. To get away from Jávea you have to go back a full six miles to the main inland road.

You leave the main thoroughfare again by another very attractive turning to reach **Moraira**, which has yet another little harbour ensconced below a sheltering headland and still more beaches south of it. These lie mostly in secluded coves and creeks divided by headland cliffs. You see them from the narrow, winding road that takes you the eight miles or so from Moraira to Calpe. The main road skirts the little town's further side. The cliffs and crags and hilly ground hereabouts have discouraged major tourist development.

Calpe however is a very pleasant, relaxed resort, much appreciated by lots of regular visitors as well as those making excursions from nearby places. It's renowned for the Peñon de Ifach, an extraordinary and vast mass of rock, sometimes compared (not very accurately) to Gibraltar, which rises no less than 1076 feet sheer from the sea just off the coast. The sandy isthmus connecting the rock's base to the shore has helped to form sandy beaches on each side of the Peñon, and the tall hotels and blocks of flats are clustered mainly at its base. The town's central attraction is the port. There's not much nightlife, but the restaurants, both those catering primarily for Spaniards and those that aim at attracting visitors, give good value. Bars abound.

Altea, almost the last of the headland's coastal towns, is another former fishing port, a lovely spot that has become a pleasant resort. White houses with red pantile roofs, divided by little cobbled streets, tumble down the hillsides above the beach. The old town's alleys make a pleasant area in which to wander. Their character's quite different from the adjoining modern development. Altea has long been popular with French visitors, who've left their mark on the town, particularly in the number and character of its restaurants. As a resort Altea's fairly peaceful. From there, through another expanse of olive groves, we come to Benidorm.

Benidorm is the Costa Blanca's great success story. In fact, many people seem to imagine it is the Costa Blanca. The town began as a tiny fishing settlement perched on a small rocky headland, with a small harbour to its south. Today, the two vast beaches of excellent sand, each a mile or so long, are both backed by vast numbers of hotels and everything else that goes to make up a modern resort. The beaches are named quite simply East Beach (Playa de Levante) and West Beach (Playa de Poniente).

One of Benidorn's special features is its compactness. All the things that holidaymakers are likely to need - food, entertainment, shops, and so on - can be found in a pretty small area inside the town's modern part. It's a notably lively place, busy with local life as well as tourism. Its restaurants include a number catering mainly for Spaniards, some with an international appeal, and some specialising in seafood. The old town forms a striking contrast to its more recent additions.

In the last twenty years or so Benidorm has become one of Spain's largest and most successful resorts. That has happened not merely because of the beaches but also through the quality of its hotels and flats, its attractively spacious and open surroundings, the excellent way that visitors are catered for not forgetting the universally popular British pubs and the excursions available. These last include day trips to Gibraltar. In short, this is very much a spot where

every member of a three-generation family group can relax and enjoy themselves, though it's worth noting that some hotels aren't particularly close to the sea.

The old fishing harbour of **Villajoyosa**, roughly six miles south of Benidorm, has developed into a minor resort, with a sizable beach on the town's southern edge. It's basically still a little Spanish fishing port, with a colourful market, lots of old fishermen's houses, and a chocolate factory. There's no nightlife, but people who start poking around in Villajoyosa tend to find they stay much longer than they plan. From here some twenty miles and a few more little-developed beaches separate you from the provincial capital, Alicante.

Its northern **San Juan** suburb itself constitutes a pretty busy resort, with rows of tall apartment blocks and hotels looking out onto a huge sandy beach. Naturally, it's a favourite playground for everyone who lives close by and less popular with international visitors than once it was. The fact that it has a large and busy commercial-industrial centre right on its doorstep may keep some people away. It's worth taking a look at Alicante. That is done in this chapter's section dealing with Excursions.

On the remaining sixty-odd miles of Alicante Province's coast only the Playa Arenales del Sol, Santa Pola, Campoamor and Torrevieja are of any real tourist interest. In a way this is extraordinary because the region contains some of the White Coast's finest beaches. But it becomes understandable when you realise that the beaches are backed by

75

empty flat land, that there are few harbours with attendant settlements, and that until relatively recently there were very few roads. It's fairly easy to build tourist accommodation onto an existing town or village, but very expensive when there's nothing there to start with. Nowadays, too, resorts have to be large enough to take at least one (and preferably several) jumbo-jet loads of tourists every week. That wasn't true of, say, Torremolinos when it first became well known.

Playa Arenales de Sol is one of this region's many resort areas that have been very little developed. There's another attractive beach stretching southward from the old fishing harbour in **Santa Pola**, a little south of Arenales del Sol. This now has a fair number of hotels and flats beside it. **Torrevieja** is rather more developed. It has hotels on the cliffs above the old town whose visitors enjoy the beaches in the coves below. It can also boast a decent selection of bars and restaurants and places for evening entertainment. It's becoming an international resort. And, still further south, **Campoamor**'s two good beaches have attracted a certain amount of building.

The rest of the coast

A few miles south of Campoamor we reach the boundary of Alicante Province and cross into Murcia's Costa Cálida. Here we've already reached one of this coast's most extraordinary features, **El Mar Menor** (the Lesser or Little Sea). It's a vast saltwater lagoon, over twelve miles long and five wide, separated

from the sea by a sandbar with a channel connecting to the sea about half way along it. Nowhere is the sandbar much more than five hundred yards wide. But there are excellent beaches both on the sandbar's seaward side and along the lagoon's inner edge. And, of course, the lagoon's sheltered water provides first-rate watersport. The landscape round about is mostly flat, with a ridge of mountains visible inland.

Several large modern-tourist residential developments of the type the Spaniards call **urbanizaciones** - the Mar del Cristal, the Playa Honda, and so on - have been built around the lagoon, especially towards its southern end. But the main international resort stands on the sandbar itself. **La Manga del Mar Menor** is wholly modern, and some of its architecture is very striking. It's sandwiched between two magnificent beaches less than a half-mile apart, one washed by the sea and the other by the lagoon, and it's noted for providing facilities for a great variety of sports. Apart from sailing, windsurfing, scuba-diving, fishing and, in the high season, water-skiing there are two eighteen-hole golf courses within easy reach. Not long ago some dedicated Brit actually also put up cricket nets and sold cricket-coaching holidays at La Manga. But that seems to have been discontinued, though La Manga's popularity continues unchecked.

At Cabo de Palos right beside El Mar Menor's southern end the coast, which has been running almost due south, becomes rocky and curves round towards the west. Twenty miles or so beyond the headland

Cartagena, built round a very sheltered bay, is a major naval base, a busy commercial port, and an industrial centre, with a large oil refinery at Escombreras some six miles away.

A further twenty miles, now by an inland road because we're in another region where the mountains reach the sea, brings us to **Puerto de Mazarrón**, another typical old fishing harbour. Sandy beaches stretch along the vast bay it stands in, and tourist development based mainly on second homes scattered over the hillsides beyond is helping to establish a very pleasant resort.

The boundary of Alicante Province reaches the sea a little beyond **Aguilas**, another up-and-coming (but internationally little-known) resort with a vast sandy beach, about thirty miles by road from Mazarrón. We're now on the Costa de Almeria. We have one more important resort to include on this eastern resort before it turns due west at Cabo de Gata.

Mojacar is the first of several small very Moorish-looking coastal settlements that we come to. The little old town consists of white-painted houses rising steeply up the slopes of a conical hill. You might easily be looking at Moulay Idriss, Chaouen, or Ouezzane in Morocco on the other side of the Strait of Gibraltar. This original settlement, built in fact by Moors, lies a mile or so from the sea. But there has been a lot of new building nearby, including not only hotels but also villas that can be bought in Britain, and holiday apartments too. Down on the coast stands one of Spain's attractive *paradores*.

Mojacar forms part of Almeria Province, which as yet has relatively few coastal resorts. The two major holiday spots on its south-facing coast are described in the chapter on Spain's south-facing coast.

Excursions from southern east coast resorts

Compared with the regions we've already discussed, this southern part of the east coast has relatively few excursion destinations. The provincial capitals of Valencia, Alicante, Murcia, and possibly Almeria are bound to attract the inquisitive. The Castillo de Guadalest makes a pleasant little outing from Benidorm. The region's orange and lemon groves are pleasant to drive through, and the large palm groves at inland Elche, some twenty-five miles from Alicante, are worth a visit. El Mar Menor is worth seeing, too, if you're not actually staying there.

But it's worth suggesting that if you want to learn something about Spain beyond the beaches, which are very much geared to keeping foreigners happy, it's worth thinking about exploring, more or less at random, some of the minor inland mountain roads. This is particularly applicable to the Sierra de Espadán north of Valencia and the mountains inland from Denia and Benidorm. You'll need the Firestone T27 and T28, of course, and someone able to read them accurately. From the viewpoint of possible excursion destinations it's worth noting that the T27, covering the extreme southern Costa Dorada and the Costa del Azahar, is unique in having absolutely no town plans or other enlargements on its reverse, while the T28 is packed tight with plans of Valencia, Alicante, Elche, Benidorm, and El Mar Menor. These are the places most people go to see.

Let's start however with the simple little run to **Castillo de Guadalest** from Benidorm. You set out through vast orchards of a variety of fruits that include not only citrus trees but also things like medlars. As you climb into the mountains you pass the little village of **Polop**, perched like Mojacar on a conical hill, and then **Callosa de Ensarria**, the region's commercial centre. Then the mountains become more majestic and bare, and you finally reach Guadalest, looking out across a valley of olives and almonds. The site is superb, with the original village perched on a ridge and accessible only through an archway cut in the rock. Unfortunately, not much remains from the distant past because an earthquake destroyed the village in 1744.

Valencia has as its main attractions a large city centre filled with tiny and very confusing one-way streets that it's hopeless for a stranger to try to drive through, a Cathedral set almost in the middle of the old central area, a number of other old churches and other old buildings, and a square, the Plaza del Caudillo, filled largely with a brilliantly colourful flower market.

The Cathedral was built on the site of a former mosque. Work began in 1262, but most of what you see today dates from the fourteenth and fifteenth centuries, with additions and alterations right down to the nineteenth century. A lot of the carving is specially impressive, and you can climb the tower that abuts onto the west front.

Churches worth seeing (if they interest you) include San Nicolás and San Juan del Mercado - St John of the Market, so-called because it stands near the market. Among other notable buildings the Lonja, or Exchange (similar to the Lonja in Palma de Mallorca), and the Palacio de la Generalidad, former meeting-place of the regional assembly, are perhaps the most important. Both date from the fifteenth century.

Like most large Spanish cities Valencia has its fair share of fine, wide nineteenth-century avenues. They are used as ring-roads today and unfortunately become terribly clogged with traffic and fumes.

Much the same applies to **Alicante**, though the town stands directly on the sea, not flanking a river like Valencia. The Cathedral of San Nicolás, built yet again on the site of a former mosque, is worth a visit. The present structure dates mainly from the seventeenth century. The Town Hall has a fine baroque facade, and the Esplanada de España beside the sea has a wonderful coloured marble pavement and lots of shady palmtrees. We've already mentioned the beach to the town's north. A good view can be had from the Castillo de Santa Barbara on Monte Benacantil, a little north of the town's centre. It occupies a strategically commanding position, where there's been a fortress since at least Carthaginian times. A lift takes you to the top, with a halfway station allowing you the option of walking part of the way up.

78

Murcia strikes many people as a specially mellow sort of town. The well-preserved old centre, located beside the River Segura, has a large area of typically tangled narrow alleys cut through by a few wider modern roads and surrounded by the nineteenth century's broad avenues. You get a fine view over the town and the surrounding mountain-ringed *huerta* from the Cathedral belfry. Murcia used to be famous for its silk-weaving. Today it has a university and is a centre for fruit-canning, wine, and commerce. The province's wines are often undervalued, but you can judge that for yourself.

Elche is basically a small industrial town that has several claims to minor fame. One is the magnificent and mysterious *Dama de Elche*, the Lady of Elche, a beautifully carved prehistoric woman's head, with an extraordinarily elaborate headdress, unearthed at La Alcudia, a mile outside the town. Unfortunately you have to go to the Museo del Prado in Madrid to see her. Another is the fascinating mediæval religious drama - or rather opera, since it's sung throughout - that recounts the Virgin Mary's death, Assumption, and Coronation performed on 14 and 15 August. You can't see that either because the public aren't admitted. You can however still see most of the town's unique palmgroves, though disease has damaged some of the trees. And the famous *Huerta del Cura* (Priest's Garden), where a carpet of flowers grows under the trees, is still there. The drive to Elche is pleasant too.

Alcoy, on the N340 road running north from Alicante, makes a useful destination for an all-day car or scooter trip through the mountains inland from Benidorm or Denia or nearby resorts. You pass the Castillo de Guadalest, described above, on the way and continue along the road you reached it by. Alcoy's position in the middle of towering mountains is magnificent, and you'll find no lack of bars and restaurants there. You can return over the Barrasqueta Pass by the main road towards Alicante and drive back north along the coast without actually venturing into the provincial capital's traffic.

Excursions will also take you to Gibraltar. But that amazing spot will be dealt with in Chapter 7.

Some highlights of this coast's year

Alicante - processions, bonfires, and bullfights for the feast of St John on 19-21 June.

Castellón de la Plana - 4-12 March (Feast of St Mary Magdalene).

Cartagena and **Murcia** have specially colourful Holy Week processions and celebrations.

Elche, as already mentioned, celebrates the Feast of the Assumption on 15 August and the two preceding days.

Valencia has festivities from 12 to 19 March, culminating in the famous procession of giant figures (*fallas*), ending up in a glorious bonfire, on 19 March.

7. Spain's Southern Coast

Apart from the tiny corner of Almeria Province, this chapter deals with Andalucia, Spain's deep south. It's an extraordinary area. It was here that the Moors held out longest and where the influence of their seven-hundred-year stay is still most strongly seen and felt. Some of their magnificent buildings have survived. So have traces in tiny villages and in these villages' very appearance.

Andalucia's a land of mountains stretching often right into the sea, of hidden valleys and villages, of splendid towns and proud people, renowned for their horsemanship, for their highly-specialised *flamenco* music and their *cante hondo* singing. For millions it's also the land of the astonishingly powerful poet, playwright, and musician Federico García Lorca. And it's where an enterprising tiny British company operates remarkable mountain riding holidays that take you into the heart of the countryside and its people.

But we must get back to mundane matters, and be precise about which Costa is which. The world-famous Costa del Sol, strictly speaking, is the coast of Málaga and Granada Provinces - from just west of Estepona to well east of Nerja. The Costa de la Luz comprises Cádiz Province's shoreline from east of Gibraltar to the mouth of the Guadalquivir. Beyond the Guadalquivir as far as the Portuguese frontier Huelva Province has relatively little tourist development. The Costa de Almeria, however, at the coast's further end, is being actively developed by the provincial authorities and can boast some very attractive resorts. Although Algeciras and Sotogrande, on either side of Gibraltar, are actually in Cádiz Province, it's almost impossible not to regard them as part of the Costa del Sol.

From Algeciras to Cabo de Gata

We'll start our survey at this stretch of coast's western end - at **Algeciras**. From one point of view Algeciras isn't a resort at all, at least not in the modern sense. It's a busy port and industrial centre, with the shortest and busiest ferry crossing to Tangier in Morocco. From a historical viewpoint however it's a very old resort, one not really based on a beach. We forget too easily that until about 1920 it was considered too, too vulgar to allow yourself to be browned by the sun. That happened only to peasants and unfortunate poor people, forced to work in the open air.

The queen of Algeciras's hotels in those days was the Reina Cristina (Queen Christina), a little outside the town to its south. The Reina Cristina's still there with its lovely garden and its little beach, some ten minutes away by car if you want to swim in the sea. Nowadays however you can swim in the hotel's pool, and lie in the sun there too. There've been other changes as well. Once upon a not very long time ago the Reina Cristina still specialised in four-poster beds for its guests. But things can't always remain the same. The Reina Cristina is still a very fine hotel.

Modern Algeciras is a pleasant town, with a fine choice of bars and restaurants and striking views across the eight-mile wide bay to Gibraltar's extraordinary clump of rock on its opposite tip. Now that the Spain-Gibraltar frontier, closed in 1969, has been reopened, ferries again cross frequently to the Rock, and there are daily departures from both Algeciras and Gibraltar to Tangier. Railway enthusiasts will know that this ferry forms part of the through rail route from Paris to exotic-sounding places in Morocco such as Tangier, Fes, Casablanca, Oujda, and even on into Algeria and south to Colomb Béchar, once the planned jumping-off point for a trans-Saharan railway line.

Algeciras is a very useful base for car exploration of the surrounding countryside twenty minutes by car or coach to Gibraltar or the very Moorish-style town of Tarifa, Europe's most southerly point, maybe an hour and a quarter to Cape Trafalgar (not considered a tourist attraction, however nostalgic it may seem to some Brits) or, in the opposite direction, to Marbella, with Cádiz, Jérez (where sherry comes from), and Ronda, all described below, providing possible destinations for full-day trips. Or of course you can cross to Tangier for the day.

The first resort beyond Gibraltar on Algeciras' eastern side is **Sotogrande**, a well-planned, custom-built modern development of hotel, bars, restaurants, nightspots, tennis courts, and luxurious villas, to say nothing of two fine eighteen-hole golf courses, a stunning new marina, a sandy beach, and masses of flowers. Sotogrande has been very carefully planned indeed, and enjoys an extremely high reputation with everyone, including the locals who flock to it as part of their weekend relaxation. It stands on flat land with lovely mountain views about fifteen miles from Algeciras, and rather less from the Gibraltar frontier at La Linea de la Concepción.

There's nothing of interest on the coastal road for the fifteen miles before **Estepona**. This is the first of a long series of modern resorts that now form an almost continuous built-up urban chain all the way to the other side of Torremolinos and Málaga.

One difficulty with this long continuous chain of resort areas is that British travel firms over the years haven't always been too careful about place-names. Several spots that were just hamlets forming part of larger local authority areas used to be separately named in brochures - Benyamina, for instance, now treated as part of Torremolinos. Mijas on the other

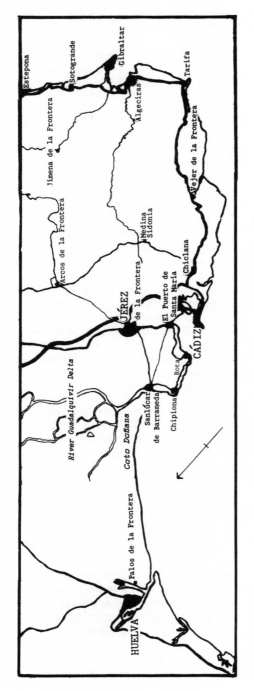

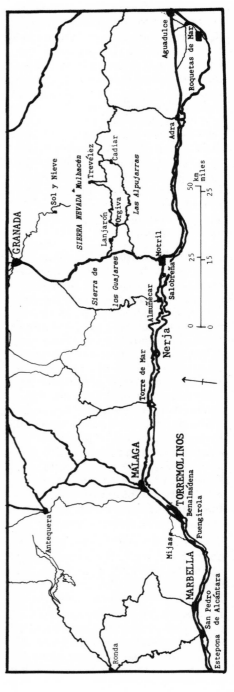

hand was once regarded as an uninteresting mountain hamlet. But its territory includes the coast below it. So it's named as a resort now as well as an excursion centre - though sometimes the old names survive. If you want precision you must consult the Firestone T29.

Estepona's based, like so many settlements along this coast, on an old village with a fishing harbour. The little port today is filled largely with smart yachts. The somewhat restricted flat land between hills and sea contains mainly holiday complexes, apartment blocks, and so on. However, there are pleasant little gardens where everyone can relax - they often contain children's swings as well as seats scattered among the buildings. There are plenty of shops, too, which cater for local folk as well as selling leather goods and other gifts and souvenirs to visitors.

The original old village beside the harbour retains its attractiveness. It includes the remains of an old Moorish castle and a two-hundred-year-old church. The two main beaches are enormously long and sandy, but not specially wide. They're backed by a mile-long promenade. Like the beach, this becomes very crowded on Sundays. Many foreign visitors however spend much of their time on the three golf courses within easy reach. The old village centre lies to one end of the resort. But distances are not great.

One point ought perhaps to be added about this stretch of coast's beaches. They're sandy alright. But it's the sort of sand that consists of extremely fine shingle grains -

excellent to lie on but no use for the kids' sandcastles.

Should you feel you'd like an original meal of fine Spanish dishes, prepared with the love that all good food deserves, try the **Yellow Book** restaurant near Estepona, right beside Kilometre 167 on the main Cádiz-Málaga coastal road (all Spanish main roads have kilometre distances clearly marked on red and white roadside stones). Its name is English, deliberately intended to recall the famous Yellow Book of the Oscar Wilde epoch. Its décor uses blowups of Aubrey Beardsley's immortal black-and-white illustrations, considered somewhat risqué in their day. The restaurant's name is also translated as *El Libro Amarillo* at the roadside for the benefit of passing Spaniards though I doubt if many grasp the complex literary-historical allusion, which possibly applies to passing Brits as well. No matter - the food's outstanding.

Estepona merges in due course into **San Pedro de Alcántara**, filled largely with residential developments. Luxurious Nueva Andalucia is among the best-known. The beach here is gritty rather than sandy, but every holiday settlement has its own swimming pool or pools. And before long you're in **Marbella**, a place that holidaymakers dream about.

It's a decidedly up-market resort - the sort of place where most people go either to be seen or to watch the people with well-known names who want to be seen. The old village lies some five miles from the more distant parts of the coast, though there are hotels close to the sea as well as inland. You can wander through its alleyways and stepped streets, past Moorish-style houses whose courtyards have in many cases been transformed into sumptuous and very attractive small restaurants. Marbella's old market is just as famous as the village's many smart boutiques, jewellers, and gift shops - and probably even better patronised.

In 1965 Marbella was still just a not very prosperous, white-painted, purely Andalusian village on the inland side of the narrow main N340 road. New tourist hotels had all been built close to the beach, and foreigners rarely even crossed the road. If they did, they got a right royal welcome.

Today there are so many high-rise buildings along this same main road that at first glance you don't even see the original white-painted village. It looks like what it also is - a busy and luxurious modern resort. Luxurious yachts fill the superb modern Puerto José Banus marina nearby, and luxurious hotels and tall blocks of flats cover all available ground. In a very short time Marbella has become where all the world knows it's smart to be seen. And a very pleasant spot it is too. It's odd to think that it used to be known mainly for its mines, blast furnaces, and fishing.

Another seventeen miles of *urbanizaciones*, flats, holiday hotels, golf courses and the like (that's what it feels like, especially when the traffic's heavy), take you through **Calahonda** (which may or may not be treated as a separate locality) to **Fuengirola**, where the atmosphere is much more relaxed.

Though it has rather more flat land behind it than most of this section of coast, the old village was spread out along the coast, with a long seafront promenade now stretching the distance of its three sizable but rather narrow beaches. Modern hotels, holiday flats, restaurants, shops, and everything else follow the same pattern.

They haven't however swamped the town's predominantly Spanish character. If you choose a bar at random you'll be more likely to find that it caters for locals than for the town's cosmopolitan visitors, even though many retired Brits have settled here. A dual-carriageway bypass avoids the narrow and always crowded main street through the heart of Fuengirola. A motorway has long been planned to run still further inland along the mountains' edge.

Los Boliches for practical purposes forms part of Fuengirola, but may be separately named in brochures. It merges imperceptibly anyway into the coastal land strip belonging to inland **Mijas**, perched on a mountain slope some way away. The area below Mijas and adjoining the beach still retains very strongly its original Spanish character. The Hotel Mijas, for instance, pre-dates the modern fashion for high-rise concrete. Local farms still flourish between the beach and the little mountain settlement. But there are also plenty of chic shops. You can take a donkey tour to the village, and when you're up there you find yourself looking down on timeless old farmhouses as well as villas with private swimming pools. Mijas has a pleasant sandy beach. But it's very different from both Fuengirola and Marbella on its western side, and also from Benalmádena and Torremolinos to its east.

As soon as you leave Mijas you're in **Benalmádena**, which some people treat as being effectively part of Torremolinos. The distance from Fuengirola is eleven miles.

Although Benalmádena continues eastward into Torremolinos with no visible seam, it's easier to treat it as a separate place. Benalmádena is essentially a custom-built modern resort based on a tiny old hamlet. The result is mainly large modern hotels set among little cobbled streets leading down to a long sandy beach. There are plenty of shops, restaurants, bars, discos, and nightclubs in Benalmádena itself, the beach is long and sandy, and the area makes a wonderful holiday spot.

Torremolinos proper is more characterful, however - if local colour's what you're after. The original village contains the Town Hall, the Tourist Office, Post Office, Police Station, Museum, market, and all the other essentials, including the main shopping street, the Calle San Miguel, and, odd though it may seem, the railway station. The railway actually runs underneath the town in a tunnel. The original settlement stood a little back from the shore, with the El Bajondillo beach below it. This is a colourful district. In parts you seem to be living in past centuries. Then suddenly you're facing a vast modern concrete block. What's odder still is that the concrete structure can just as easily be an office block as a new hotel. There

are plenty of small park areas scattered among the buildings, too. The total distance from the further edge of Benalmádena is about four miles, and frequent buses link the different districts of Torremolinos-Benalmádena.

The fisherfolk of thirty years back and more lived in La Carihuela, a little west of Torremolinos village. Some of the old houses still remain, and the area retains some of its original character though now dominated by tall hotels and blocks of flats. Upper and Lower Montemar (Montemar de Arriba and Montemar de Abajo) abut onto both La Carihuela and Benalmádena. Benyamina, east of Torremolinos' original village, has been pretty completely absorbed into its now much larger neighbour, and is filled almost wholly with modern resort building. The total distance from Benalmádena is about seven miles.

Wherever you stay in the Benalmádena-Torremolinos-Benyamina complex you can find virtually everything you're likely to need within easy reach. This applies especially to things like self-catering supplies, bars, restaurants, and so on. It may be worth noting however that the best shopping area is generally reckoned to be in the old village of Torremolinos, and that Montemar is considered the disco and nightlife centre - which certainly doesn't mean that it's the only part containing nightspots. Apart from all that, not the least of Greater Torremolinos' advantages is that it's very close to Málaga Airport. Interestingly enough, it's also close to the **Parador del Campo de Golf**, which the Spanish government built many years ago to encourage tourism (!) in this area.

A word about golf courses in this region ought perhaps to be added here. They're a special topic, requiring specialist discussion. Here we can only note that they're pretty numerous and said to be of very high quality. Various companies specialise in golfing holidays and should be able to sort out all your needs if you're keen about the game. But if all you want is a casual round or two with some of your friends you should have no difficulty in getting to a course wherever you choose to stay. Green fees are reasonable and club hire is usually possible. Your hotel will certainly be able to advise you or to get you the necessary information. Much the same applies to serious tennis in this region. A number of the tennis schools have a very high reputation.

From Torremolinos it's only about ten more miles to Málaga, the province's capital and yet another of Spain's fine cities, and to some extent still a holiday resort (it's dealt with under Excursions, below). It has one or two modest hotels in the town centre. The better ones, which people use for vacations, are mostly strung out along the Paseo de Sancho, the main road leading eastward out of the town below the hill called the Gibralfaro (Lighthouse Hill), with a fine Moorish fort on its lower slopes. This road, incidentally, forms part of the N340, which runs all the way from Cádiz to Barcelona. It's a sort of minor imitation of the USA's famous coastal Highway 1.

For thirty-two miles east of Málaga the N340 runs between mountains and sea, with **Torre de Mar** the only settlement of any size. Torre's partly industrial, but in part also a resort with a good beach. Most of its visitors are Spanish, though it also offers holiday flats.

Nerja on the other hand, at the end of the thirty-two miles, is a major international holiday spot. It's built mainly on land beside the mouth of a little river, with a peninsula jutting some way out to sea. The view southward down the straight coast used to be so famous from the peninsula's tip that it was christened *Balcón de Europa* (the Balcony of Europe), and the name still appears on many maps. Modern building unfortunately has rather obscured the view.

Nerja however remains a very pleasant place for holidays. The old town, with its collection of narrow lanes and white houses, grew up at the base of the rocky promontory, and now has newer building around it. This includes holiday flats as well as hotels. Several beaches, none very large, are spread around the town. Caves discovered in 1959, which penetrate over half a mile into the mountainside about two miles east of Nerja, attract a lot of visitors.

For thirty miles east of Nerja the coast road takes the form of an extremely attractive corniche, which is also, unfortunately, very wearing to drive. It twists and turns continuously, rising and falling along the cliffs and between the pinewoods, and providing very attractive views over the usually dark blue sea. It's forced inland at points, one of which is **La Herradura**, a small modern resort built on a terrace of flat land below the cliffs carrying the road.

At **Almuñecar**, a little over five miles from La Herradura, the road drops briefly into a small plain containing what appears to be a very well laid out modern town. Rising above the town however you'll see a conical hill crowned with a Moorish castle and covered with what might easily be the original Moorish houses were it not for their outward-facing windows. It's a rather fine sight. Beyond the town that you see from the main road there's a considerable number of hotels and residential holiday estates, and some very good beaches. The town's original name, incidentally, going back beyond the Moors to Carthaginian days, was Sexi. Don't draw faulty conclusions if you see hotels, restaurants, or nightclubs carrying the ancient name.

Almuñecar, whose current name indicates very clearly the present settlement's Moorish origin, lies about halfway along the Nerja-Salobreña stretch of corniche, with an exciting mountain road, very narrow in parts, cutting inland to Granada. Bear it in mind for excursions.

At the corniche road's eastern end you come to **Salobreña**, one of the most characterful little spots on this part of the coast. It's very obviously based on yet another conical gleaming-white once-Moorish village, with an old Moorish castle perched at its peak. It stands on the edge of a plain filled with a vast expanse of dusty sugar cane that extends a long way inland. A very attractive small modern hotel was

built a few years ago a little west of Salobreña, on low cliffs overlooking a charmingly quiet beach. It's decidedly pleasant to stay at. But if you fancy something more traditional, there's a fine little *posada*, one of the ancient inns that catered for travellers using horses, mules, or donkeys, in the old town's steep main street. This one however has converted its former stables for other uses.

One of the posadas' most likeable characteristics is that they feed you so well and for such low prices. Maybe it's because the inns are always run by the *señoras*, presumably while their menfolk work in the fields - or wherever they're employed nowadays. The riding holiday company based in nearby Orgiva once got a message from a posada *señora* asking them to come and see her urgently. They feared some terrible disaster, or an impending row. But no. The lady merely wanted to say how worried she was that the horseriders never seemed able to finish all the food she prepared for them. She took eating very seriously.

Motril, on the further side of the plain from Salobreña, is a port and sugar-processing centre which has its own beach and a nine-hole golf course. Granada, with the magnificent Alhambra Palace southwest of it, lies forty miles inland by a mountain road that finally comes into view of Granada at the summit of the Puerto del Sospiro del Moro - the Moor's Sigh Pass, allegedly the last tribute of the departing Moors when they were finally driven from Granada on 2 January 1492. In actual fact, they hung on until 1609 in Las Alpujarras, the Happy Lands, the mountains which have Orgiva as their centre and a host of white Moorish-Andalusian villages scattered through them.

Beyond Motril the road narrows and runs between mountains and sea for some thirty miles before reaching flatter land and entering the Province of Almeria. **Adra** is almost the only settlement of any note. It's basically just a small port. Beyond it the road turns inland over fairly level land heading straight for the provincial capital, Almeria, which is dealt with in this chapter's Excursions section.

Two new resorts began to be developed rather more than ten years ago on the coast a little before you reach Almeria. **Roquetas de Mar** lies on flat land between two extensive sets of saltpans about five miles south of the main road to Almeria. The resort is attractively based on a small older village whose harbour is still a fishing base, and whose market is still a colourful occasion. Though Roquetas isn't very large there's a certain amount of cheerful nightlife and an eighteen-hole golf course next door to the resort. Intended for Spanish as well as foreign visitors, the resort area includes two well-designed modern shopping centres and a number of colourful buildings clearly based on Moorish patterns.

Roquetas is fundamentally a restful place. Excursions are limited in the main to bus trips into Almeria and hiring a car with which to explore the inland mountains on Andalucia's western edge. This involves fairly tough driving, and

you'll need a good map - Firestone's T-series unfortunately fails to cover this corner of Spain's coasts. For most people however Roquetas' excellent big beach will be all they want. It must be made clear, though, that the sand here is not the sort that youngsters can build sandcastles with. Nor is it fine enough to be blown into your eyes in strong winds.

Aguadulce lies six miles away, tucked into the angle where the main road joins the coast. It's newer than Roquetas but not quite as peaceful because of the busy main road. Some hotels lie on the further side from the shore. The beach itself however is really tip-top - though, as at Roquetas, the sand isn't of the sort that children most enjoy playing with. And there's plenty of it. Aguadulce itself is a very tiny place, and essentially Spanish in character.

Resorts of the Costa de la Luz

West of Algeciras - we're going in the opposite direction now - the coast becomes mountainous. The road runs well inland for some fifteen miles, and there are no coastal settlements till you reach **Tarifa**, a decidedly Moorish-looking town, with its walls and horseshoe gate. It's Europe's most southerly settlement, barely eight miles from the Moroccan coast. On clear days you have a good view not only of Africa's coast but also of the long Rif Mountain range parallel with it. Don't be frightened of going through the gate and exploring the town. You won't upset anyone. Tarifa's not really an excursion destination, but it's worth a stop during a drive to, say, Cádiz or Jérez or further afield. The town itself, with its white houses and tangled lanes, is a good introduction to what you see almost throughout North Africa. It boasts a small harbour, a castle, and a causeway taking you out to the rocky Punta de Tarifa, Europe's ultimate southerly point.

A lonely but attractive thirty-mile drive taking you gradually onto flatter terrain brings you to **Vejer de la Frontera**, whose name introduces us to a historical fact that dominates this whole region and gives it a lot of its distinctive character. It was called *La Frontera* because for centuries it was in fact the frontier between the Christian north and the Islamic-ruled south. Many place-names here have had *de la Frontera* added to them. Arcos de la Frontera and Jérez de la Frontera (the sherry town's full name) are among the best known. Vejer de la Frontera, like Mojacar, Almuñecar, Salobreña, and other old once-Moorish towns, rises gleaming white on a conical hill. It is famous for its stork colonies. A roadsign just past Vejer says coldly 'Cabo Trafalgar'.

Another more colourful twenty miles or so bring you to **Chiclana**, on the edge of the extensive marshes surrounding Cádiz Bay. If you're bound for Cádiz, fork left at the T-junction. If not, keep right. You've already had an excellent view of all-white Cádiz on its narrow peninsula with the sea on one side and its vast bay, now divided by a causeway and bridge, on the other. There's a brief account of Cádiz town in the Excursions section towards the end of this chapter.

You can get to the Costa de la Luz's three main resorts by following the old main road towards Jérez - not the relatively new motorway - and making a circuit from **El Puerto de Santa Maria**, the port that sherry is shipped from and a pleasant place to stay at. It has a sort of solidly-established, mellow atmosphere, as well as a pleasant beach and a good choice of restaurants and bars, many of them geared more to Spanish than to foreign visitors. If you turn right there towards Jérez, be very careful not to get into the town's complex of narrow streets. Take the ring road (*circonvallación*), and fork left almost as soon as you join it.

This road brings you quickly to **Sanlúcar de Barrameda**, some fifteen miles away. Sanlúcar's a very attractive town and a flourishing resort, popular with people from both Jérez and inland Seville. The motorway from Seville links with the Jérez ring road, making the sixty-mile run from the big city very fast, and the very pleasant beach extremely crowded at weekends.

Sanlúcar's interests aren't by any means limited to tourism. It serves also as headquarters for the winegrowers and producers of Manzanilla, a wine matured in the same way as sherry (see the section on Jérez, below). The *bodegas* (wine cellars) are all located in the old town, on the hillside below the castle. It's even claimed that it's Sanlúcar's salty atmosphere that gives Manzanilla its special flavour, and that a barrel of *fino* (thin dry sherry) brought from Jérez turns into

Manzanilla if it's left to mature in Sanlúcar.

Apart from this bit of vital information you may like to know that the Moorish castle at the top of the town was given to the Dukes of Medina Sidonia (one of whom later commanded the Armada) as long ago as 1264, and that Sanlúcar, in the days when ships were tiny by our standards, was a major port. Columbus started his third expedition from here in 1498, and from here Magellan set out to sail round the world in 1599. The town lies right at the mouth of the mighty Guadalquivir, facing into its vast and mostly marshy delta. A fair proportion of this land is occupied by the world-famous Coto Doñana nature reserve, not open to the public except with special permission.

Chipiona is a rather quieter family resort built onto a town located on a headland a little over five miles west of Sanlúcar. Near the town the beach has been stabilised with breakwaters. But the sand extends most of the ten miles to **Rota**, the most modest of the modest Costa de la Luz's resorts. It has a beautiful pine-fringed beach on its northern side, and an even larger one in a wide bay to its south. The old town centre, perched on its hill and ringed by ramparts, seems to have altered little since mediæval times.

One or two more places along the coast before you reach the River Guadalmina and the Portuguese frontier act as leisure and holiday resorts for the Sevillanos. But none is likely to be of interest to foreign holidaymakers unless they happen to be staying with Spanish friends in the region.

One little town however will nevertheless be holding the whole world's attention in 1992. This is **Palos de la Frontera**, on the broad eastern arm of the Rio Tinto's delta. It was from here that Genoese-born Columbus set sail for the discovery of America in 1492. Preparations for celebrating the fifth centenary of this monumental event were already well in hand when this was written in June 1987.

The coast from the Portuguese frontier as far as the River Guadalquivir's west bank opposite Sanlúcar de Barrameda belongs to Huelva Province. From Sanlúcar to just short of Estepona it forms part of the Province of Cádiz.

Excursions from Costa del Sol and Costa de la Luz resorts

Some of the excursions possible from resorts along this southern coast are obvious and almost unavoidable. You need to be desperately unenterprising to stay in Algeciras, for instance, looking straight across the bay to the extraordinary vast lump of mountain that is Gibraltar without feeling an urge to go and explore it. Other exciting trips aren't obvious, but they're decidedly worthwhile.

We'll start at the coast's eastern end with **Almeria**. It's a fairly typical large and prosperous Spanish city, very easily reached from Aguadulce and Roquetas. And it has a number of attractive features. One of them is the Alcazaba, the ancient Moorish fortress on the top of the hill dominating the town. Moorish castles of this type are a feature of many towns along this coast. But this is the first we have come across.

The word, incidentally, is the same as the Arabic word we usually write *kasbah* (*al* = the), and it means fortress or citadel. The citadel areas of North African towns - that is, the part of the town where the final defence would be mounted in the event of an enemy assault - are often full of tortuous narrow alleys like the rest of the town. Algiers' *kasbah* is like this, and because of the attention it attracted after the French conquest of Algeria in 1830 people have tended to imagine that the word kasbah refers to this sort of town layout. It doesn't. Many kasbahs are in fact isolated castles set in lonely countryside.

The word *Alcázar*, also taken from the Arabic, is usually applied in Spanish to Moorish palaces or former palaces. In modern Arabic *ksar* indicates a fortified (or formerly fortified) village. *Medina* means town - and traditional old Arabic towns (European ones, too, for that matter) were always a maze of tangled alleys. *Alcántara* means bridge. All this may sound a bit pompous. But these names recur frequently in Southern Spain, so it may be as well to get them right now.

Almeria's Alcazaba dates from the eighth century, and can be visited. It was badly damaged by an earthquake in 1522, but the Tower of Homage and the mosque are worth seeing. Remains of encircling ramparts run towards a second hill, the Cerro de San Cristóbal, formerly topped by a later castle. Once they enclosed also the city's oldest part below the hill, still called (surprise! surprise!) Almedina. Some of its old alleys still survive, and lead you to the Cathedral, built in 1524 on the site of a former mosque. It's particularly interesting that at that date corsair raids and Almeria's openness to attack from the sea were still sufficiently violent and frequent to force the builders into making a fortress of the Cathedral. But that doesn't prevent it being also an attractively designed structure.

Once, of course, the shore below Almedina just sloped down to a little beach, where raiders could easily land. A very pleasant tree-lined park has been built on the embankment constructed later to provide deep-water berths for larger vessels. At its western end, close below the Moorish castle, the old fishing quarter of La Chanca remains very attractive. The modern commercial harbour lies mainly east of the park, with some good beaches beyond it. And Alicante can boast some elegant shops and restaurants in its main street, the Paseo del Generalísimo.

If you take either of the roads leading northwards out of Almeria, the N340 towards Vera and Mojacar or the N324 leading to **Guadix** and Granada (the x in Guadix isn't pronounced: it's almost the only non-phonetic word in Spanish), you'll get good views of Almeria Province's desert-like landscapes. Parts of *Lawrence of Arabia* were made here and the region is in heavy demand as locations for Westerns. If you go all the way to Guadix and beyond you'll also find perfectly comfortable houses hollowed out of the soft rock. It sounds pretty primitive but in fact isn't. The doors often have smart brass knockers, and tv aerials stick out of the rock above them. These cave dwellings around Guadix have become fairly well known among foreign visitors. But this isn't the only region where they're found in Spain.

Granada and the **Alhambra** (the name *Kalat Alhambra* means Red Castle) are the region's, and indeed one of the world's, best-known excursion destinations. The magnificent Alhambra is the obvious main centre of attraction. But it shouldn't be forgotten that Granada itself is also an impressive town that has a good deal to offer.

Apart from good shops, the Cathedral and various other churches, the Alcaicería, the former Moorish silk merchants' quarter, has been reconstructed as a tourist precinct, complete with craft and souvenir shops (in Moroccan towns the equivalent area is usually called the *kisseria*). The Albaicin hill area, the Moors' first settling place and the area they retreated to after being driven from the Alhambra, still retains all its ancient alleys. The view from in front of its St Nicholas' church over the Alhambra and the Generalife Gardens above the Alhambra palace is magnificent - especially at sunset. And at Sacromonte the caves occupied by gipsies can still be seen. This used to be just the gipsies' own territory, where they danced and sang for their own entertainment. But it has become a major tourist day resort.

As for the Alhambra, if you don't take a coach excursion and get put down close to the entrance you'll find parking your car and struggling up the steep slope the palace stands on pretty tiring - especially in the middle of a hot day. But the Alhambra is worth almost any effort. The only problem is that you need about a week to absorb its atmosphere and take it all in.

It takes some time to attune yourself to Islamic architecture if you're not already accustomed to it. And even more to appreciate the subtleties of different styles. But if you can manage just to relax and slowly absorb the amazing skill of the artists and architects who produced such superb, intricate surface decorations and such beautifully proportioned rooms and patios and buildings on which to display it you'll begin to wish you had much longer to spend here.

You go through a whole series of rooms and courtyards, and it's impossible even to begin to describe them here. For a first visit, anyway, you'll probably find it best just to wander slowly through (preferably without a guide talking at you) and to try to take in no more than the place's atmosphere. Details can come later - a lot later - on subsequent visits.

One slight problem is that parts of the Alhambra began to be 'modernised' in 1526, making them a bit of a jumble, particularly as the work was only finally completed a few years ago. If you want to know about all this you can buy perfectly adequate guides in English at the entrance. A point worth remembering perhaps is that a century ago much of the Alhambra might just have been left to rot if the

American writer Washington Irving hadn't fought for its preservation. He's still honoured as the building's saviour.

The Generalife, above the Alhambra, served as the Kings of Granada's summer palace. Its gardens, laid out in typically formal patterns, were intended for relaxation, and were also designed to be at their best in July and August. Unfortunately, parts of the gardens sometimes appear less well kept than one imagines they were in Moorish times, and they're crammed in July and August with tourists from what seems every country in the world. And these people all seem to be forever pointing their cameras and saying in a babel of tongues: 'No, dear, stand over here where I've got you in front of those roses. No, dear, here'.

There are other Moorish gardens, less attractive and much less magnificently sited perhaps, which are nevertheless a lot more conducive to the sort of peaceful contemplation such gardens were deliberately designed to encourage. But don't let this put you off enjoying the Generalife gardens. One movement of de Falla's enchanting *Nights in the Gardens of Spain* suite for piano and orchestra describes them well - as they were in his day.

If you spend time enjoying Granada and the Alhambra you may also find it worthwhile taking the mountain road southwest of the town up to the **Sol y Nieve** (Sun and Snow) ski resort high in the Sierra Nevada. The mountain range's highest peak,

Mulhacén, over 11,000 feet high, looks down on the resort. It's one of Spain's finest and most successful spots for winter sports and it's delightful in summer too. A very rough, unsurfaced track continues beyond the resort over Mulhacén's summit and into the country beyond.

In a totally different yet closely-related, nearby setting anyone who wants a glimpse of this region's striking countrysides can hire a car and drive a circuit of fascinating little white villages based on **Orgiva**. You reach Orgiva by taking the Granada road from Motril and turning off after ten miles.

It looks like a small modern Spanish town as you approach it. But to the left of its main square, behind the modern banks and shops, you'll find a district of little white houses and narrow streets which still show traces of patterned cobbles dating from Moorish days. And in this area's tiny main street, named after General Franco, you'll find the old *posada*. It's called the Posada Pescado, the Fish Inn, because for centuries fish carried up from the coast by mule was sold in its courtyard.

If you take the road north (you have to go back from the square and turn right) you can drive through a whole succession of little white villages - Pitres, Portugos, Trevélez, Jobiles, Berchules, Cadiar, and Torvizcón. Bear right at every fork till you get back to the large bridge over the River Guadalfeo which you crossed as you were approaching Orgiva.

You can eat simply but well at the

posadas in Pitres, Trevélez, and elsewhere. Trevélez is particularly interesting. The village is famous throughout Spain for its snow-cured ham. The snow comes from the Sierra Nevada, at whose foot it stands. The bridle track running north from Trevélez over the Puerto del Lobo (Wolf Pass) is the highest in Europe, and Trevélez itself, well over five thousand feet above sea level is Europe's highest village occupied all year round. And it's a very attractive spot, whose *posada* stands conveniently beside the main road. This was surfaced about ten years ago, and the circuit recommended is now popular also with Spaniards making coach excursions.

If you want a close-up view of one of these villages, park your car wherever you can - car parking's as big a problem in Spain as everywhere else - and walk straight on downhill out of the little main square's further lefthand corner.

You come after a time to the ancient *posada* almost at the old village's edge. Beyond it you can follow the muletrack that is even older than the posada. It goes along the bottom of the valley for a time, and then begins to climb. And you'll see that the track has been built with vast stone blocks clearly designed to last for centuries. This was once a major route for hill farmers bringing equipment and maybe provisions up from the coast. You'll still see them riding their mules out to work in the fields.

But perhaps you should be warned that this is a fairly tough drive, not too easy for anyone with no previous experience of mountain driving. But it makes a wonderful long day out. A little north from Orgiva, incidentally, just before you rejoin the main Motril-Granada road if you're heading inland, you go through Lanjarón, the town which supplies mineral water to nearly all Spain.

Our next excursion point along the coast is **Málaga**. It combines the attractions of a lively, fashionable provincial capital and communications centre with those of a historic city and minor resort. Charter planes fly into its airport from all over Western Europe all year round, and ferries ply regularly from its harbour to Ceuta on the Moroccan coast and to other Mediterranean ports. Málaga can also be very easily reached by road from all the holiday spots on the Costa del Sol's western side - Torremolinos in particular is only eight miles away. It's about thirty-two miles from Nerja on its eastern side and perhaps fifty from Almuñecar.

The town's worth a visit. Its shopping centre is the Calle de Marqués de Larios, west of the Cathedral with an area of narrow old streets between, and the Plaza José Antonio at Marqués de Larios' inland end. The Cathedral, whose decorations include the arms of Philip II of Spain and Mary Stuart, stands somewhat west of the hill topped by the Gibralfaro, with a small square church that was once a mosque on its inland side and pleasantly laid out gardens a little way away towards the harbour. The traffic around the gardens is unfortunately heavy and smelly almost all day. The roads round it form part of Málaga's main through route.

You reach the Alcazaba, the old fort on Gibralfaro hill's lower slopes, through fortified gateways and Moorish gardens where honeysuckle, bougainvillea, and jasmine grow plentifully. The Alcazaba itself is now a museum of Moorish art. You can walk on up to the ramparts at the summit of Gibralfaro (the name means Lighthouse Hill), from where you have a lovely view over the town and its harbour. You can also drive up to the *parador* beside them. The gardens inside the ramparts are open to the public too.

The artist Picasso was born in the Plaza de la Merced, less than three hundred yards from the Alcazaba (northwest). Between his birthplace and the Cathedral the Museum of Fine Art (Museo de Bellas Artes) has some examples of works by him and also by his teacher Muñoz Degrain and other Spanish artists. Between the main streets of this central part of the town Málaga has a mass of narrow alleys that are always attractive to explore.

The little white village of **Mijas**, in the mountains directly inland from Fuengirola, makes a short excursion that everyone enjoys. It's a very attractive and colourful spot, full of shops, boutiques, bars, and restaurants, and with some lovely views over the coast.

A much longer inland journey takes you to the remarkable little town of **Ronda**, nearly 2500 feet above sea level. Its older part, the so-called Ciudad, occupies a spectacular position at the top of sheer six-hundred-foot high cliffs, and it's divided in two by the high-level Puente Nuevo (New Bridge)

spanning the rocky, precipitous River Guadalevin gorge. It's called 'New' only because of much older Roman and Moorish bridges, of which traces still remain.

The Ciudad, south of the bridge, was once the capital of a small Moorish kingdom. Its streets are a mixture of modern building, mediæval Spanish styles, and original Moorish. Parts of the Moorish town wall still survive. The attractive church of Santa Maria Mayor stands in a very pleasant small square and contains some fine polychrome (ie, painted and gilded) statues. Other survivals include part of the Moorish King's palace, the tower of a former mosque, remains of the Alcazaba and its beautiful gateway, and more. Making a thorough exploration of the Ciudad is strenuous - its streets are cobbled and anything but flat - but well worth the effort.

Not the least of Ronda's attractions is its famous bullring - the first to be built in modern style and elegantly constructed entirely in stone. It was three generations of a Ronda family, the Romeros, spanning the years 1700-1839, who gave Spain the bullfighting traditions accepted by everyone today and the *corrida*, as it's called, its present form. Before the Romeros a different form of bullfighting, the *corredera,* had been the privilege only of the mounted gentry.

Gibraltar makes a fascinating all-day trip from Costa del Sol resorts (three days, because of the distance involved, from most of the Costa Blanca). It's an extraordinary place - a mountain some 1400 feet high rising sheer from sea level, with a thousand-foot cliff - the North Face -

soaring vertically on its northern side, and ending in an area of flat land thirty feet or more above the sea at its southern tip.

During the siege begun by the Spanish in 1779 long passages were laboriously cut by hand high up in the North Face to enable guns to be brought to bear on the Spanish attackers. They are well worth visiting. The modern artificial harbour and Gibraltar town lie on the Rock's western side, with much of the space now filled with tall modern buildings. The original naval harbour, Rosia Bay, south of the town, now looks almost like a toy pool. It was here that the ship carrying Nelson's body (bent double in a barrel of rum) put in to give the world the news of the Battle of Trafalgar and the Gibraltar Times its one and only all-time scoop, appropriately remembered on the walls of London's Press Club.

Gibraltar is said to have got its name from a corruption of the Arabic Djebel Tarik - Mount Tarik - so-called from the name of the invading commander. Clear evidence of the Moorish occupation exists in the form of the Moorish Castle (actually a square tower) halfway up the hill above the old town, in the remains of Moorish baths, and in the huge defensive wall running right to the Rock's summit ridge some distance south of the town. If you're feeling energetic, try climbing all the steps along this wall. It will give you some good views, and also a good idea of the Rock's fascinating plants. Birdwatching in the migration seasons is also worthwhile.

The Apes' Den, where the Rock's famous and very mischievous Barbary apes are regularly fed by an Army corporal and the sick ones given attention, lies a little up the slope, not far from St Michael's Cave (you can drive up there or take the cable car), one of Gibraltar's innumerable limestone caverns, large enough to be used as a concert hall for symphony concerts. Whatever you do, don't let the monkeys grab your camera or anything else you're carrying. If they do you'll never see it again, and you'll feel a right charlie telling your insurance company that a monkey stole it, and you know because you saw him. On the flat land at Gibraltar's southern tip the indomitable British troops used to play cricket on a ground of gravel with a matting wicket. It wasn't too funny if you fell over running flat out to stop a boundary.

You can drive all round Gibraltar by car and travel much of it by coach. There's also a cable-car to take you to the restaurant on the summit ridge. From here you can look down onto the steep eastern side's huge area of painted corrugated iron sheets that collect rain and dew to be stored in vast underground cisterns for the Rock's water supply. You can also see tiny Catalan Bay and the modern hotels and other accommodation built above the narrow but pleasant beaches.

A road runs right round the Rock, and its airport is an artificial platform constructed across the narrow isthmus connecting it to the mainland, in what was strictly defined as neutral land by the treaty of 1713 that ceded Gibraltar to Britain. You actually have to drive

On Mount Mulhacen's northern slopes, high above the
Alhambra, skiers revel in the snow at the Sol y Nieve
(Sun and Snow) resort.

The Alhambra's intricate Moorish patterns belong to an age when people had time to stand and stare.

Salamanca's Plaza Nayor is one of Spains many architectural jewels.

The most impressive of Spain's innumerable relics of Roman builders' skill, the Aqueduct at Segovia.

across the runway to reach the Spanish frontier. But delays because of planes landing or taking off aren't too frequent.

During World War II vast subterranean shelters, ammunition stores, HQ command posts, and even a huge underground hospital were excavated under the Rock. Some of this space is now being used as an auditorium for a superb laser show telling Gibraltar's story. The thirty-minute show runs regularly through most of the day, so you should get a chance to see it. But there's a lot more to Gibraltar than can ever be recounted here. It's a pity that no decent book exists to tell you about the Rock and its story - and about the extraordinary part it has played in Britain's history.

But we must be on our way. Tarifa, the Moorish-built town at Europe's southernmost point, which you pass on the road to Cádiz and Jérez, has already been mentioned. Also Vejer de la Frontera. **Cádiz** itself deserves a visit, if only for its historical associations and for its magnificent site. But the town itself is cramped and rather claustrophobic, and parking is near-impossible.

The English in Elizabeth I's day spent a lot of time trying to destroy the city. Drake boasted that he had 'singed the King of Spain's beard' when he burnt a number of ships anchored there which were intended for the invasion of England. That didn't prevent the Armada sailing from Cádiz a year later, in 1588. Nor Essex and Howard from sacking the town eight years after that. Nor repeated subsequent English attacks. But the city still stands there, gleaming and magnificent above the blue Mediterranean.

Much of it is filled with the usual tangle of narrow old alleys. But a fine promenade looks out to sea on its southern side, and the Cathedral beside it is worth a visit. Its Treasury has a notable collection of plate.

Jérez de la Frontera lies inland from Cádiz. British attempts to pronounce this fascinating old town's name have given us the word 'sherry'. Part of the town retains its old fortifications but the ***bodegas*** of the numerous sherry firms are the city's main attraction. These huge, cool, white-painted single-storeyed warehouses are the places where sherry matures in long banks of vast barrels.

Every morning from Monday to Saturday all the firms keep open house to visitors, except during lunch hours. All have guides to show you round and explain the very complex processes of sherry-making. All the larger firms - you will recognise the well-known names - have English-speaking guides. The British connection is in fact strong and centuries-old.

One of sherry's fascinating differences is that the barrels in which the wines mature are never completely emptied. Former vintages are blended with new ones to preserve exactly the same flavour and quality. In some cases the blending is done in containers that have been neither moved nor emptied for a century or more. Another odd point is that the fermenting juice seems largely to make its own decisions as to which type of wine it turns into - the thin dry *fino*, golden medium *amontillado*, sweet deep-coloured *oloroso*, or very sweet *dulce*. At least, this is what the vintners say. Production processes today are kept under strict scientific control. Nevertheless a huge amount of human skill and judgment goes into making really fine sherries. Visits to *bodegas* normally end with tastings. But you can't usually buy the firm's products on the spot.

Beyond the *bodegas* Jérez is a fascinating old town, with attractive squares, elegant old houses, and fine churches. The surrounding region's rolling hills, mostly covered with vineyards, and its gleaming white villages have a distinctive character of their own.

Should you be staying in one of the Costa de la Luz's resorts **Seville** is a very easy run. But we can't deal here with this magnificent city. It will have to be content with a rather brief outline in Chapter VIII.

There are however two further places that excursions from the Costa del Sol and the Costa de la Luz (and also some resorts rather further away) can go to, and they're not quite as different from the places we've just been seeing as you might expect. One is **Tetuan** in Morocco. You reach it by the ferry which crosses from Málaga to the Spanish town of Ceuta (Sebta in Arabic) on Morocco's Mediterranean coast. Tetuan is only a short drive inland.

It occupies a delightful position on a mountain buttress overlooking the valley of Oued (River) Martin, which flows down to the Mediterranean seven miles away. Until 1956 it was the capital of Spain's Protectorate in Morocco (France governed - or tried to govern: it was a distinctly unruly place - the country's other half). As a result the New Town looks almost totally Spanish, with most street names in Spanish. But when you go into the *medina*, as the old Arabic parts of Morocco's towns are always called, you feel you've really moved back a few centuries, even though by Moroccan standards Tetuan's *medina* is pretty uncomplicated and easy to find your way round.

With a guide to lead you, you can see the former slave market, the silversmiths' street, the dungeons where Christian prisoners were kept, several mosques (though you're unlikely to be allowed inside), the *kasbah* which dominates the town, a nineteenth century *fondouk* (merchants' inn), and the fine *mellah* (former Jewish quarter), also dating from the nineteenth century. But you can enjoy yourself almost as much if you just wander through the *medina*. Since you're bound to get thirsty during the day, this is a good opportunity to try the Moroccans' favourite thirst-quenching drink - mint tea. It's made with fresh mint and sugar - a lot of both - and it's very good indeed.

When you return from Tetuan you'll feel you've really been in a different world, and you'll understand a little better Southern Spain's ubiquitous Moorish remains.

Our other possible excursion destination is **Tangier**, also in Morocco. Ferries cross frequently from Algeciras and Gibraltar, and there are air links from Gibraltar. The little white *medina* climbing up the hill from the port was once the whole of Tangier. A century ago, in fact, even the port didn't exist. Visitors were carried ashore after being brought to the beach from their steamers in rowing boats. Today the medina is an appendage to the modern town that spreads east along the coast and over the inland hills rather than the other way round. But the medina, the old royal palace, the busy markets, and the English church - Tangier was for a long time a favourite spot with expatriate Brits, and was actually a British possession for a brief period - are all worth seeing.

8.   Hidden Spain

If you've taken some of the excursions to inland and other towns that have been described, or have pottered through the countryside by car or scooter to a few slightly out-of-the-way villages - or maybe have just read the preceding chapters' descriptions, which hopefully are lively enough to give you a decent idea of them - you'll realise that the Spain of the resorts and their beaches is very different from the Spain that's 'hidden' from most people - but only because they don't bother to discover it. If you really start to explore you'll find it a country that repays you a thousandfold for the efforts you put into getting to know it. And nowadays, thanks to modern roads and fly-drive holidays and the like, that's no longer a real effort.

To describe briefly regions that between them really require a dozen guidebooks - one could easily be filled just with Madrid, or the Basque country, or the Picos de Europa - isn't easy. This chapter can do no more than give you a taste of what remains to be discovered.

Andalucia

We'll start more or less where we left off - with Andalucia and the deep south. If you've tackled the journey inland to Ronda or made the

Alpujarras tour from Orgiva you'll have glimpsed something of Andalucia's character. It's a region of extraordinary high, crumpled mountains, with sunbaked, half-green valleys running in all directions and a feeling, much of the time, of utter remoteness. There are few woods or even trees (other than olive groves and occasional orange orchards) to give a feeling of warmth, however hard the sun may shine. It's a harsh, unrelenting landscape.

You'll sense this side of Andalucia even more strongly if you drive on from Ronda to Jérez through the fine old town of **Arcos de la Frontera**. On the map much of the route looks like main road. On the ground it's rather different, despite newly-constructed highways.

Arcos is a lovely spot, a typically Moorish white town climbing high up a mountainside's steep slope, with a magnificent view from the little square outside the church at the top (and nowhere to park, of course: that encourages you to do it on foot). There's a pleasant *parador* on the square's other side from the church, too.

But Arcos is only one of many rather similar Andalusian towns. **Medina Sidonia, Moron de la Frontera, Jiména de la Frontera**, and other small spots are worth a visit too. So are the tiny villages of the **Sierra de los Guajares** - Guajar Fondón, Guajar Farragüit, Guajar Alto, and the rest - directly west of the main Motril-Granada road. That applies also to **Yegen**, where an annual festival of local traditional folk music is held, and many similar spots beyond Cadiar, which was mentioned in the suggested circular drive from Orgiva. Seen from a distance, all could easily be North African settlements. Indeed, in origin they were.

But Andalucia has fine big towns and forests and vast modern artificial lakes designed for irrigation and hydro-electric power as well. Málaga and Cádiz and Granada have already been mentioned among the towns. In many people's eyes however white **Cordóba** soars above them all in its fairylike appeal.

In Roman days Córdoba was the birthplace of the philosopher Seneca (4 BC-AD 65), tutor to the unhappy Emperor Nero (who later ordered him to commit suicide) and till the nineteenth century one of the Western world's most influential philosopher-authors. Also of the Silver Age epic poet Lucan (AD 39-65), another of the young Nero's companions. You can enter the town by an impressive long Roman bridge crossing the broad River Guadalquivir that's still very much in use, though considerably restored at different periods.

And what a town it is! At the bridge's northern end you're in the heart of the former Moorish settlement, with the vast mass of the Cathedral directly opposite you. They call it the **mezquita** (mosque),

which is exactly what it still is - an enormous mosque supported on 850 massive columns, retaining virtually all its original decorations and its **mihrab** set in the wall facing Mecca. It was built over twelve hundred years ago, in 786.

Starting in the thirteenth century a large Christian sanctuary was built in the very middle of this mosque, and alterations continued for over three hundred years. Today what you see is a massive enclosed choir area similar to those of many Spanish Cathedrals with vast expanses of dark carved choirstalls and surrounding panels. It makes an extraordinary contrast with the colourful mosque that it stands in.

Beyond the **mezquita** the old Jewish quarter, the Judería, is just as colourful, with its dreamlike little alleys lined with bright white houses and their flower-filled patios. Remains of the Alcázar of the Caliphs of Córdoba stand in a lovely Moorish garden barely two hundred yards west of the mezquita. Today it's a mixture of Moorish patios, fountains, and baths, Roman mosaics, and a Christian king's palace built in the fourteenth century.

About four hundred yards away on the Cathedral's other side you'll find an arcaded square (plaza) once used for **correderas**, bullfights of the type normal before the Romero family of Ronda changed everything. At **Medina Azahara**, four miles or so west of Córdoba, you can see the well-restored remains of a tenth century Moorish palace. And all around the city's ancient centre lie modern industrial suburbs. But who wants to think about them when you can dream of past glories in the lovely heart of this stupendous town? Ancient Córdoba wasn't only a beautiful place. It was also a major seat of learning, where the Moor whom we call Averroes and the Jew we know as Maimonides taught before the ancient universities of Paris, Bologna, Oxford, or Salamanca even existed.

You can easily get carried away merely by thinking of Córdoba. Some people however feel just as strongly about **Sevilla**, to give the town the Spanish form of its name. Its history is even more extraordinary, for it was not only a Roman provincial capital but also for a time the capital of a Visigoth kingdom before the Moors arrived in 712 AD. Under Moorish rule it became the capital, late in the twelfth century, of the Almohad Sultan, Yacoub el Mansur (1184-99), whose territory included all Morocco and beyond.

It was el Mansur who built the famous Koutoubia Tower in Marrakech, the Hassan Tower in Morocco's present capital, Rabat, and the Giralda Tower in Sevilla. Closely resembling Rabat's Hassan Tower, the Giralda stands over 230 feet high and was once a minaret. It rises beside the Cathedral constructed where the Giralda's mosque once stood. The name means 'weathercock', and was given to the tower in the sixteenth century when the top storey lantern and revolving bronze figure of Faith were added to the minaret. Sevilla fell into Christian hands in 1248, when the Alhambra in Granada was still not in existence. Not till 1401

was it decided to knock down the old mosque and build 'a Cathedral so immense that everyone, on beholding it, will take us for madmen'.

That's roughly what we have today. It really is an enormous building, and extraordinarily ornate, which can be a bit overwhelming. Columbus's tomb is as vast and ornate as anything else in the building - not surprisingly, since his discovery of the New World brought undreamed of prosperity to the town.

Once Sevilla was a famous port. The Florentine Amerigo Vespucci, who tried to prove that Columbus (Cristóbal Colón in Spanish) had made a mistake and who succeeded only in giving his own name to the continent that his rival had discovered, set out from here. But the Guadalquivir had silted up by the early eighteenth century, and Sevilla's prosperity declined.

Nevertheless, the town still contains the splendid Alcázar Gardens, just southeast of the Cathedral. The Alcázar itself - or, rather, the **Alcázares Reales**, the Royal Alcázars, since the buildings include several Moorish and royal palaces - display outstanding examples of mudejar art, the work of Moslem artists done for Christian employers. The Barrio de Santa Cruz (Holy Cross Quarter), directly east of the Cathedral, rivals Córdoba's Judería, and the Archivo General de Indias (Archive of the Indies) has a unique historical collection illustrating Spain's arrival in the New World and the discoveries made by Spaniards there.

One of the most striking buildings however is the extremely ornate eighteenth century Royal Tobacco Factory (Fábrica Real de Tobacos - tobacco was once a royal monopoly) located just south of the Alcázar. Built round ten courts it houses part of the university today. Once it was the main setting for Prosper Merrimée's novel which Bizet turned into the opera Carmen.

The peak of Sevilla's year is Holy Week, the period leading up to Easter Day which is celebrated throughout Spain, but nowhere as dedicatedly or as sumptuously as here. People from all over the world flock to see the colourful processions. Hotel prices rise steeply, and rooms even so are very difficult to come by.

If you want a more complete picture of Andalucia you must travel eastward to towns like **Jaén** and **Ubeda** and to the mountains and forests of the **Sierra de Cazorla**. Like Granada, Córdoba, Seville, Málaga, and all the rest, Jaén and Ubeda were once Moorish towns, though they contain fine aristocratic houses from later days as well. Wolves are still not yet extinct in the Sierra de Cazorla. Much of its forest land has been designated a nature reserve. But the public can wander there along marked paths. Like Jaén and Ubeda, Cazorla possesses a well-appointed *parador*.

Immediately north of Seville and Córdoba the **Sierra Morena**, running in a long ridge from the Portuguese frontier to Central Spain, cuts off inland Spain from Andalucia, from the flat lands around the deltas of the Guadalquivir and the Tinto, and from warm Mediterranean air. Its name means 'the Dark Mountain', and it's a pretty empty region. Only two main roads cross it the NIV from Granada to Madrid and the N630 going almost due north from Seville up Spain's western side.

If we follow the NIV we come to a remarkable and remarkably attractive region, with Madrid at its heart. At 2120 feet above sea level Madrid claims to be Europe's highest capital. Its position in the centre of Spain's vast land mass makes it excruciatingly hot in summer and bitingly cold in winter. Excellent skiing can be enjoyed barely twenty miles to the northwest in the Guadarrama Mountains. But Madrid is also an exceptionally lovely and impressive city. It takes its name from the Moorish fort of Majerit, reconquered by Christian forces in 1083, and formally made Spain's capital in the sixteenth century.

Madrid and Central Spain

Built on mainly gentle hills sloping down to the River Manzanares, **Madrid** today is a city of magnificent wide avenues, well laid-out eighteenth and nineteenth century districts, and rapidly-expanding new industrial and residential suburbs. The main places of interest, however, lie in the old city centre around the square called the Puerta del Sol (Sun Gate - the actual gate disappeared centuries ago).

In an area consisting almost entirely of narrow little streets dating from the city's earliest days you'll find the delightful vast Plaza Mayor (Main Square), surrounded by seventeenth century houses and closed to traffic, the massive eighteenth century Royal Palace (Palacio Real) and its famous Armoury (Armeria), the Convento de las Descalzalas Reales (usually translated Convent of the Poor Clares), innumerable other fascinating old buildings and, of course, a mass of delightful small bars and restaurants.

The Descalzalas Reales were a religious order founded by a daughter of the Holy Roman Emperor Charles V in the early sixteenth century. The name really means 'royal barefoot ones', but since the order consisted largely of royalty and aristocracy their families and friends heaped wealth of every sort on the order and their superb building and magnificent collection of religious art is now on public display. Their twelve seventeenth century tapestries based on cartoons by Rubens and the painting by Titian entitled Caesar's Pence are specially famous.

The Royal Palace lies on the western side of this central area of Old Madrid. To the east lies the superb Prado Museum, one of the world's great art galleries, with the famous Retiro Gardens (Jardines del Retiro), cool and shady, close behind it. The vast Prado Museum displays over six thousand works of art of virtually every age and many countries. In front of it the magnificently broad Prado Avenue (Avenida del Prado) allows all Madrid's drivers to indulge their skills to the full. You may be able to manage cars weaving in and out of four-lane

traffic. When fifty-seater coaches start doing this it's probably less hassle to pull round the corner and wait till the rush hour peters out.

The Prado's a long way from being Madrid's only worthwhile museum, and the Retiro Gardens aren't its only open space. You'll find an excellent Folk Museum (Museo del Pueblo), and another devoted to Folk Decorative Art. Others deal with the Americas, bullfighting, contemporary art, and so on. And beyond the Royal Palace, on the other side of the town's inner centre, the Parque del Ouest (West Park) provides a very pleasant place to stroll in and relax - and also to eat: attractive restaurants with pleasant views line the park's main promenade.

You can easily spend a week or two exploring the region round Madrid. Excellent coach tours take in the region (as they do Andalucia) and one enterprising firm also offers fly-drive weeks based on Madrid - though a week is hardly long enough if you want to explore the region thoroughly. If you want to see Madrid itself you can buy 'city break' package stays.

Barely twenty-five miles south of Madrid by the NIV you reach **Aranjuez**, whose name is known to millions through the blind composer Rodrigo's *Concierto de Aranjuez* for guitar and orchestra. He named it after the lovely gardens of the royal palace there, where he spent many happy days during his honeymoon and thirty subsequent summer holidays.

The present palace, like the gardens, is open to the public. The buildings go back to the sixteenth century, but are mainly of the eighteenth, while the furnishings are as they were a hundred or so years ago. The garden's divided into several parts, including an English Garden whose elms were specially imported shortly before the Armada. There's also a smaller eighteenth century palace in it called the Casa del Labrador (Ploughman's House), rather similar to the Petit Trianon at Versailles.

From Aranjuez it's a speedy twenty-mile run to **Toledo**, a dream city if ever there was one. Perched on a hill almost completely surrounded by the River Tagus (Tajo in Spanish), it has changed remarkably little since one of its most famous citizens, El Greco (1548-1625), painted his renowned *View of Toledo*. A hilly road round the river loop's outer edge brings you to viewpoints (where you can park) that give you almost exactly the same view looking down into the town that El Greco painted. The view has hardly changed.

Most of Toledo is built in striking white stone, and the narrow streets are often paved with the same material. Lined with houses that are frequently extraordinarily elegant and beautiful the streets are anything but flat, and their steepness adds considerably to the town's attractions. Sightseeing by coach is out of the question, and a car is almost useless. You have to walk.

The approach to the Cathedral down the Calle de Comercio, one of the city's main shopping streets, is lovely beyond words. The fine Cathedral itself is exceptional. It contains notable fifteenth and sixteenth century choirstalls, paintings by El Greco, Goya, Bellini, Van Dyck, Titian, and others, and a lot else worth lingering over. But that's only a beginning.

The charming sixteenth century house where El Greco lived has been restored and transformed into a museum containing, among other things, a number of his paintings. The mudejar church of San Roman contains a fascinating Visigoth museum - the town was for a time capital of a small Visigoth kingdom (for mudejar art see Chapter 9).

Outside the fifteenth century church of St John of the Kings (San Juan de los Reyes) chains taken from Christian prisoners freed after the liberation of the town from the Moors are on display. The Church itself got its name through being built to receive the bodies of Ferdinand and Isabella, the 'Catholic Monarchs' (Los Reyes Católicos) who drove the last Moors from Spain, though they were in the end buried in Granada. And of course there are endless reminders of the fame that Toledo's fine steel blades once enjoyed in the form of innumerable souvenir daggers and the like. But the town's main attraction is just its site and its streets.

If you're really bent on exploring this central area of Spain your next port of call should be **San Martín de Valdeiglesias**, about fifty miles away by the N403 road heading towards Avila. Outside the town an extraordinary group of bulls carved in granite, known as the **Bulls of Guisando** (Los Toros de Guisando), have stood guard for thousands of years. They may be the work of ancient Celtic sculptors.

The gaunt **Sierra de Gredos** (Gredos Mountains) begin just west of San Martín. The range rises to 8502 feet in its centre. It's a fine region for mountain walking, mountaineering, and shooting - or just for quiet exploring.

The lovely and historic town of **Ávila** lies under thirty miles beyond San Martín. Its eleventh century walls are still intact - over thirty feet high, reinforced by 88 towers and bastions, and entered by eight gates. In 1085, with Salamanca and Segovia, both dealt with below, it formed the fortified Christian front line against Islam. You can still follow part of the walls' sentry path (closed weekday afternoons October-May).

The Cathedral, several other churches, and a number of secular buildings are all worth exploring in Ávila. But merely walking through the old town is delightful. For many people the name of Ávila is best known as the birthplace of St Teresa. Her letters, especially those to her spiritual adviser St John of the Cross (see Chapter 9), occupy an important place in Spain's literature. And her struggle to re-establish strict monastic discipline at a time when laxity was becoming the norm played a vital part in preserving Spain's strongly Catholic culture.

From Ávila you can drive the eighteen-odd miles to Villacastín and then cut back southeast towards Madrid to see the enormous monastery-palace of **El Escorial** and the **Valley of the Fallen** (Valle de los Caidos), Spain's grandiose

memorial to the dead of all sides in the 1936-39 Civil War.

You reach the Valley of the Fallen first. Situated in a magnificent valley filled with rocky crags and pinewoods in the heart of the Sierra de Guadarrama, a little over thirty miles from Madrid, it consists of an enormous church carved inside a vast rock surmounted by a huge cross. The church's nave is over eight hundred feet long (compared with St Paul's Cathedral's five hundred feet), and the cross five hundred feet high.

El Escorial is on the same sort of scale. It's mentioned in the section dealing with Architecture in Chapter 9. Most of its magnificent rooms and courtyards can be seen in company with official guides.

If you continue a bit on the main road towards Madrid and turn north at Villalba you drive through the seven-thousand-foot **Navacerrada Pass** ski resort, high in the Guadarrama range, and ten miles later reach **La Granja de San Idelfonso**. It's a little royal palace often likened to Versailles, although it lies nearly four thousand feet above the sea. Fine gardens surround it.

From here you simply continue on your way to yet another lovely town, **Segovia**. It's one more of Spain's ancient fortified cities. Unlike Ávila, however, its walls aren't quite complete, and it's famous as much for the magnificent Roman aqueduct just outside the town that's still carrying water across a deep valley as for its own buildings. The wonderfully impressive aqueduct is 92 feet high and 728 long.

Segovia's location, the Alcázar (last rebuilt in the nineteenth century, with nothing Moorish in its present appearance), and the streets, squares, and churches of the old town are all delightful.

If you're still not tired of driving, or have decided to extend your stay for another week, try leaving Segovia by the road leading northeast, the N110. Follow it as far as its junction with the NI, where you turn south towards Madrid. Turn south, cross the Somosierra Pass, and take the first tiny road to your left, eight miles or so from where you joined the NI. If you follow the bends of this road at the foot of the Somosierra hills to the north, you'll come about a quarter of an hour later to another tiny turning on your left, with a village out of sight from the main road barely half a mile along it.

Even today this village, so close to the main road, seems extraordinarily remote. And it seems almost to belong still to the Middle Ages. The first thing you see is a series of paved threshing floors, where grain was once threshed by men and women wielding flails, cascading down a hillside in front of you. An extraordinary story attaches to this village. A lecturer at Madrid's Complutense University whose speciality is the history of church estates in the seventeenth century discovered it in a seventeenth century document.

At a certain moment various church holdings were transferred to the crown, and royal commissioners rode out to tell the villagers. They came to this village and made their announcement. 'Good heavens', said the villagers, 'Does that mean the Moors have left?'. The Moors had been gone six hundred years and no one knew.

A number of towns west of the NI, that can be reached easily from Madrid, are also worth exploring. They include **Sigüenza** and **Alcalá de Henares**. But reaching them from close to the Somosierra Pass requires a good deal of complicated cross-country driving. Perhaps it would be better to leave them for another trip.

A little south of these spots the flattish region known as **La Mancha** provides a high proportion of Spain's better known wines. It's also famous as the setting for Don Quixote's adventures, and worth visiting if only to follow in the mournful knight's steps. It's easy enough to view the windmills at places like **Mota del Cuervo**, **Campo de Critana**, or **Consuegra** as giants that should be charged and destroyed. Easy enough, too, to imagine the poor Don's adventures in the region's modest village inns.

West and north of Madrid

But we must move to regions west and north of this central part of Spain. Though by no means devoid of mountains, a large part of this area is typical of the relatively flat tableland that in Spain is always called the *meseta* (the word in fact means just tableland). Because it's flat you tend to think you're at or near sea level. But in truth you're several hundred feet above it at even its lowest points. It's a harsh land to work, though improvements such as huge stretches of irrigation made possible by enormous new dams are now being made. Historically, it has provided many of Spain's emigrants to America and elsewhere.

But it contains also a number of very striking large cities. A few of these are in the southern part of our region, known as **Extremadura**, the 'land beyond the River Duero', so named in the days when the struggle against the Moors dominated people's minds. The modern Province of Extremadura lies in fact a fair way from the river, and this chapter deals with a much larger region, from the Sierra Morena in the south to the Picos de Europa and the Cordillera Cantábrica in the north. For the ordinary visitor, not able to wander around for months, the towns provide most interest.

Extremadura proper's three main towns, **Bádajoz**, **Mérida**, and **Cáceres** have been fortresses for thousands of years. Bádajoz, indeed, guarding the mountainous frontier with Portugal (which was ruled by Spain from 1580 to 1668), facing fortified Elvas and Estremoz on the other side, was continuously fought over right into the nineteenth century. Mérida derives its name from its Latin form - Colonia Emerita Augusta, a settlement of Roman legionary ex-servicemen designed to 'pacify' the locality. Cáceres still preserves the inner Old Town's walls, with a fine array of knights' houses inside them.

All three towns are delightful to wander in, not least because they're well removed from the ordinary tourist routes. Here you can see Spain as it really is. It's virtually impossible for a stranger even to think of driving in Bádajoz. Walking through the tangled narrow streets you can enjoy them and also the town ramparts' remaining parts to the full. In Old Cáceres, even though the rampart towers erected by individual noble families were lopped by order of Queen Isabella in 1477, you can still feel that you're in a late mediæval fighting town. The houses nearly all carry their noble builders' coats of arms (essential for recognition when most people were illiterate), and everything has a purposeful air.

Mérida still shows plentiful traces of its Roman past, with two Roman bridges spanning the rivers Alberregas and Guadiana, remains of a racecourse, two aqueducts, temples, theatres, and much else. The Moorish Alcazaba built over a thousand years ago to defend one of the Roman bridges is still there. And strolling through the mediæval old town's streets is a wonderful relaxation.

The little town centre of **Trujillo**, thirty miles due east of Cáceres, is a gem of sixteenth and seventeenth century architecture. It lies on the NV, the direct road from Madrid to Mérida, Bádajoz, and Lisbon.

Going straight north on the N630 from Mérida brings you eventually to **Salamanca**, roughly sixty miles northwest of Ávila and one of the most beautiful of all Spain's towns. It's particularly famous for its Plaza Mayor (Main Square), built for the town in the early eighteenth century by Philip V in gratitude for wartime support. A model of Salamanca's Plaza Mayor is one of the great delights of Barcelona's Pueblo

Español museum.

Salamanca's so-called Schools Square (Patio de las Escuelas), containing the original University (there are two others today) and some of its ancient schools and hostels, is in fact even more glorious than the Plaza Mayor. It contains Spain's best collection of the highly-decorated Gothic architecture known as 'plateresque' (from its resemblance to silversmith's reliefs - *platero* means silversmith). The main entrance to the University is particularly fine. Other outstanding buildings include the 'New' Cathedral (it was completed in 1560 and stands alongside its romanesque predecessor) and a whole series of other churches and houses.

But we must move out of Salamanca Province into León and Old Castile (Castilla la Vieja), both of them ancient independent kingdoms. **Valladolid** almost rivals Salamanca in the glory of its architecture - and if you can pronounce the name the way the locals do you're really beginning to speak true Castilian Spanish (see the Language Guide in Chapter 11). In Valladolid the dominant style is 'Isabelline', the immediate forerunner of plateresque, taking its name from the fifteenth century Queen Isabella. The patio of the San Gregorio College is magnificent, but it's not by any means alone among Valladolid's buildings. Yet again the town's old centre consists of narrow streets and alleys centred on a fine Cathedral.

The town of **León**, eighty miles northwest of Valladolid, is a little different. There's an old town centre here too, and part of its tenth century fortifications still stand. But the area inside, as at Aosta in Northern Italy, is only that of a single Roman legion's original camp, such as campaigning troops laid out every night. The town's great pride however is the Hostal de San Marcos, whose facade is over three hundred feet long.

The present building dates from the sixteenth century, when it was designed as a monastery. But its site was connected with the Knights of the Order of St James from the twelfth century on. The Order was instituted to protect the pilgrims who came not only from Spain but also from France, the Low Countries, Germany, Scandinavia, and Britain to make the long, laborious journey to the shrine of St James (Santiago) at Compostela.

The Apostle James, it was believed, had sailed to Spain to spread the gospel and had been buried there. But the whereabouts of his grave had been forgotten during the Moslem invasion. In 844, a mysterious knight on a white charger who had given valiant help to a small group of Spaniards attacking a body of Moors near Logroño was identified as St James (called thereafter Santiago Matamore - St James the Slayer of Moors). When a group of angels revealed the whereabouts of his earthly remains to a shepherd a shrine was erected worthy to receive them, and gradually all Western Europe began to look on a pilgrimage to what is now the Cathedral of Santiago de Compostela as second in importance only to a pilgrimage to

Jerusalem. Both were expressions of international Christian solidarity against Moslem invaders.

León was a vital stopping place along the Pilgrims' Road (or rather roads) to Compostela, the **Camino de Santiago**, which came gradually to be equipped with hostels where the travellers could stay, chapels where they could pray, hospitals where their ailments could be tended, and even paved sections where the going would be easier over difficult terrain. We'll have a chance to consider a bit more closely some of the remains of this ancient highway stretching right across Northern Spain and crossing the Pyrenees into France at three points when we look at Santiago de Compostela itself.

In the sixteenth century the Hostal de San Marcos took its present form as a large monastery. Today it is an extremely sumptuous hotel, rivalled only by the really superb **Hostal de los Reyes Católicos** in Santiago de Compostela itself, dealt with later in this chapter.

Apart from San Marcos, León's little Cathedral, tucked into a corner of the original small fortified Old Town, is a specially attractive building, with some excellent and very large stained glass windows going back up to seven hundred years. And the old part of the town, around the Cathedral, is attractive, too, though the twentieth century and its incessant noise is all too apparent all around you.

Burgos, some eighty miles east of León as the crow flies, was an even more important staging post on the road to Compostela than León. The two towns are connected by no very direct road today, and if you want to follow the Pilgrims' Road you have a good deal of cross-country driving to do. But Burgos today is a major point on the busy NI that connects Madrid to the French frontier at Hendaye, at the Pyrenees western end.

Burgos is also an extraordinarily pleasant little town. Motorways bypass it today, and even the NI keeps south of the not very wide River Arionzón, while the town centre lies mainly along its opposite bank. The main bridge crossing the river still has the fourteenth century tower designed to protect it on the further bank. Beyond the tower you'll find the pleasant Plaza del Rey San Fernando, with convenient cafés facing the fine Cathedral's southern side. Burgos is a flourishing university town, and not the least of its attractions (and of this little square too) is the number of lively (and very well-behaved) young people usually in it.

Beyond the Cathedral the hillside slopes down to form a quite shallow valley, giving the old part of the town an elongated layout. Exploring its streets is enjoyable: the old town centre, the porticoed Plaza José Antonio, forms the setting for all public festivities, notably the Holy Week and Corpus Christi processions. Sections of the original town did however spread across the river. The present Archaeological Museum occupies a very pleasant building south of the stream, the Casa Miranda, which was the Cathedral canons' residence in the sixteenth century. The bus station stands almost opposite it today.

When Ferdinand I united the crowns of León, the Asturias, and Castile in 1037 Burgos became the capital for the campaigns which by 1083 had freed Madrid. It grew rich on tribute from minor Moslem rulers, and a number of wealthy monasteries were founded around it in subsequent centuries. The Convent of Las Huelgas Reales, the Miraflores Carthusian Monastery (Cartuja de Miraflores), and the Hospital del Rey (King's Hostel), where pilgrims were given shelter, all lie within three miles of the town centre.

The legendary Rodrigo Díaz, better known as El Cid, was born six miles from Burgos in 1026. He was buried in 1102 in the Monastery of San Pedro de Cardeña, seven miles east of the town. But his remains were transferred to the Cathedral in 1942. His magnificent deeds as Castile's champion against the infidels, celebrated in epic ballads that have survived the centuries, are legendary. In actual fact he was quite capable of fighting for either side, according to whichever provided most profit. Inevitably, he himself is now exploited for profit in his turn. You'll see reminders of him everywhere. A house said to have been his now operates as a very pleasant restaurant.

The northern hills and mountains

When you're in Burgos the Atlantic lies only about seventy miles to your north at the lovely town of Santander. But the long range of the **Cordillera Cantábrica** rises between you and the sea. Mostly the land altitude is so high in Spain that you don't much notice the mountains unless they rise over five thousand feet. They mostly seem to be just slightly higher land, long rolling hillsides, usually fairly bare of the trees that grow mainly on lower ground. That's true of much of the Cordillera Cantábrica - except for a notably higher clump lying west and a little south of Santander.

This is the magnificent **Picos de Europa** range, where the landscapes suddenly seem to have changed completely. The valleys become abruptly green and well-wooded, with trees that include walnuts, cherries, apples, and medlars, as well as most of the woodland growth we're accustomed to in Britain. In atmosphere, the little towns resemble those of most high-mountain regions, whether Switzerland, Austria, Italy, or even New York State's Adirondacks. Building details may be different, but the way the houses and shops all sit tight-gathered at the foot of steep slopes topped by jagged peaks, as though for mutual shelter and warmth, is the same. And between the greener valleys and open mountain slopes the Picos de Europa offers a succession of narrow defiles and rocky gorges linked by passes rising to four and five thousand feet.

You can drive right round the range's central heights on a triangular route from **Panes** in the northeast to **Potes** by the N621 and on over the high San Glorio pass as far as the N621's junction with a minor road, the C637. Here you turn north for the Ponton Pass, Oseja de Sajambre village, the gaunt devastation of the bare, six-mile-long Los Beyos gorge, and the little town of **Cangas de Onis**. The rest of the journey is eastward on the N6312, taking you back to Panes, where you started the trip.

The total distance on this tour is only about 125 miles. But you'll find you need at least two or three days if you're to enjoy it properly. For one thing you'll certainly want to drive along the Deva's green valley from Potes to **Espinama** and up as far as the modern *parador* at **Fuente Dé** (Source of the Dé), nestling comfortably nearly 3500 above sea level below the range's highest peak, the 8688-foot Torre Cerredo. Once up by the parador, the cable car taking you a further 2500 feet up to a magnificent cliff-edge viewpoint that's also the starting-place for wonderful high-mountain walks is pretty well irresistible. So you might as well spend the night - or several nights - at the parador itself, or in hospitable Potes, or in a valley campsite near Espinama.

If by now you've fallen in love with these mountains - it happens to lots of people - you'll think about hiring one of the jeeps that are available locally for trips over the rough mountain tracks that take you into really uninhabited territory (apart from one or two very remote mines and power stations), where you stay in mountain refuges and explore the range's high interior on foot. If not, you can continue to, say, Cangas de Onis.

From here you simply must make another, shorter diversion - to **Covadonga**. For Spaniards, this is virtually holy ground. In 718 a local leader who claimed descent from

the Christian Visigoth kings raised a rebellion against the Moorish invaders. Four years later he thrashed a force aiming to wipe out him and his troops. It was the beginning of the seven and a half centuries needed to expel the Moors. A vast basilica was built to commemorate the victory in 1886. It's the scene of magnificent celebrations every year beginning on 8 September. They include a festival of the local shepherds' ancient folk music. In 1918 the area was declared a National Park - Spain's first.

If you ever think of exploring this area seriously you'll find the Firestone T21 map is a must. It shows you very clearly not only all the roads you'll need, but also all the mountain paths and jeep tracks (*pistas para jeep*), the viewpoints, and the mountain refuges, together with a panorama sketch of Picos de Europa summits, town plans and street gazetteers of the nearby big towns of Gijon, Santander, and central Oviedo, and drawings and explanations (in Spanish only) of the region's typical country buildings.

Difficulties of terrain have prevented ski resort development in the Picos de Europa. The northern mountains' most important winter sports centre is at the top of the **Pajares Pass**, thirty-five rather mountainous miles south of Oviedo and well west of the Picos themselves.

The northern coast

We must leave these mountains and hurry on to Spain's northern coast. First however we'll stop for a look at one of Spain's most astonishing old villages, **Santillana del Mar**. The T21 will tell you that at Panes you're only an easy forty-mile drive from this extraordinary settlement.

The name really means St Juliana of the Sea, though the sea, a bare four miles away, seems very remote once you're inside the village. So does virtually everything else, for Santillana amazingly consists wholly of fifteenth, sixteenth, and seventeenth century noblemen's houses, built of stone and roofed with well-weathered red pantiles, along with the much earlier collegiate church where St Juliana is buried. The whole place is laid out in a ring based on two main roads.

Most of the houses still carry their builders' crests. Very few of their exteriors have been noticeably altered, and more recent building is extremely scarce. Santillana takes you vividly back three hundred years, cobblestones, red tiles, flowered balconies, and all. One of the ancient houses makes a beautifully modernised *parador*. Others serve as restaurants. And, of course, you've the inevitable vast choice of twentieth century souvenirs.

The whole coastal area between mountains and sea hereabouts is riddled with caves which in prehistoric times were used as homes. Those at **Altamira**, little more than a mile from Santillana, are world-famous. The first prehistoric rock paintings and carvings ever discovered were found here in 1879. Those of the Dordogne, in France, became known only twenty years later. Altamira's oldest carvings are believed to date from

around 25,000 BC, and the paintings from 15-12,000 BC.

The very attractive peninsular town of **Santander**, with flower-filled gardens and fine beaches on either side of its headland, lies little more than twenty miles from Santillana and Altamira. Car-ferries connect it with Britain, and the main southbound road to Spain's interior and to Madrid and the south, the N623, takes you through Burgos over the Puerto del Escudo (Shield Pass), 3500 feet above sea level. An alternative, the N611, slower and more winding and also longer, lets you see Valladolid and Segovia on the way.

The **Santander Coast** (Costa de Santander), on either side of the provincial capital, includes a number of resorts that are very popular with holidaying Spaniards. They'd be just as well frequented by North Europeans were it not for the wetter, less certain summer weather. We're in the Atlantic, not the Mediterranean climatic zone. While summers can be extremely hot, a little light rain is also always possible. It's known locally by the delightful name of **chirimiri**. But Spaniards accustomed to the meseta's harsh summer heat aren't likely to be discouraged by it. The green of the countryside round the resorts makes them very different from those on Spain's Mediterranean side.

Castro Urdiales enjoys a striking site in a wide, mountain-ringed bay with a good beach, and has the reputation of being Northern Spain's most attractive coast resort. It's still however a fairly busy port. On 3 August it celebrates a festival of its own with a battle of flowers, parade of decorated floats, and fireworks. **Laredo**, unlike its US namesake, also combines a busy fishing harbour with a strikingly lovely position, a massive beach, and a flourishing tourist area. It's a very attractive town.

Santoña, tucked in under a headland protecting a wide, well-sheltered rocky bay, is mainly another fishing base. But **Noja**, further along the coast, has three fine beaches, one rather cut up by small reefs but the others excellent, and it's developing fast. West of Santander, the main resorts are **Comillas**, once a royal residence and today the seat of the Papal University, and **San Vicente de la Barquera**. Apart from a vast beach the latter has some fine old houses in the very colourful town, an extremely long bridge carried on twenty-eight arches over the cliff-lined estuary-inlet the town stands on, and a pleasantly arcaded Plaza Mayor.

By now, incidentally, we have reached the beginning of the region of the *rías*, the hill-lined estuaries that get larger and rockier as we travel towards Spain's northwestern corner and its west-facing coast. They vary from small and pleasant - one always associates them somehow with sun sparkling on blue water - to huge and spectacular, rather like Brittany's *abers*.

The **Costa Verde** (Green Coast), lying wholly in the Province of Oviedo, begins beyond San Vicente and extends for 180 miles on either side of the large industrial centre and busy port of Gijon. The best-known resorts of the Green Coast, some of it lying directly north of the Picos de Europa, include **Llanes**, **Ribadesella**, **Luarca**, and a considerable number of smaller places. The road linking them is narrow and winding, and becomes more and more difficult the further west you go. But it's a fascinating experience to explore this region. It's very unlike everthing you're accustomed to think of as Spanish.

Llanes is notable for its tall fishermen's houses and its numerous sandy beaches, and Luarca for its slate-roofed white buildings as well as another fine sandy beach. Ribadesella - the name means Sella Bank - stages an extremely popular kayak race on the River Sella every first Sunday in August.

Spain's far northwest

When we finally cross into **Galicia** we have to abandon the coastal road (unless time is absolutely no object) because of the deeply-indented and often vast *rías*. The countryside has also changed pretty well totally. It's still extremely hilly. But flowers seem to grow everywhere, especially geraniums, and the fields are green. Farm holdings are traditionally often very small. Maize, potatoes, rye, and grapes are among the main crops, and large stretches of land are used for pasturage. Further south you'll also find huge stretches of mountainside thickly sprinkled with fragrant broom, wonderful to drive through when it's in bloom - provided you're not allergic to its pollen.

The buildings are different too. Lots of the little cottages could easily have come from English villages. There are still plenty of small *horreos* to be seen, granaries raised on stone stilts to discourage rats. Many farmhouses run to several storeys, with the farm animals housed on the ground floor. And out in the wilds you'll still occasionally come across simple shepherds' dwellings whose roofs are thatched with broom. The *gállego* dialect spoken here is very close to Portuguese, with most -s- sounds pronounced as -sh-. The earliest known settlers were Celts (the Celts penetrated almost everywhere in the ancient Western and Near Eastern world), and the bagpipe, a sure sign of Celtic penetration, is among the region's most popular folk instruments.

Two of Spain's most important ports, Corunna (La Coruña in Spanish) and Vigo, are hidden away in Galicia's vast, well-sheltered *rías*. Given the rise and fall of the huge Atlantic tides and the storms that sweep across that ocean they need to be. It's a very different world from the Mediterranean.

La Coruña is a busy seaport and and extraordinarily attractive town. Yet its history was one of almost regular warfare up to the end of the nineteenth century. The Armada set out from here in 1588 after Drake had destroyed Spain's first great fleet in Cádiz harbour the previous year. In 1589 the English attacked and nearly destroyed the town - the plaque to the woman who raised the alarm can still be seen. In 1809 the English under Sir John Moore defended the city unsuccessfully

against Napoleon's forces. Throughout the nineteenth century it was a base for liberal risings. But today it's a peaceful and colourful spot, famous mainly for old houses with typical glazed balconies overlooking the harbour, and for its second century Hercules Tower, one of Europe's earliest lighthouses. The tiny 'Ciudad', as the formerly fortified old town is called, still retains its ancient cobbled streets and quiet squares, perched on the peninsula that shelters the port.

Vigo, way down in the south of this west-facing coast, is set in an even vaster and better-sheltered bay. While the town itself is less attractive than La Coruña, its surroundings of rocks and cliffs and pine-covered hill slopes are magnificent. The old town and the fishermen's quarter close to the modern harbour are colourful. Three excellent beaches stretch southwards from the town.

Many other coastal towns tucked away in Galicia's deep inlets are well worth seeing - places like **Pontevedra** and **Bayona**, for instance, where Columbus put in in 1493 to give the Old World its first news of America. The long-established luxury resort of **La Toja** also deserves special mention. It operated a casino and a private nudist beach long before such things were considered even thinkable in Spain. It has a wonderfully picturesque and secluded position on its own island.

The pearl of this whole region however is one of Europe's loveliest and most historic towns, one which many people think gets far less attention than it deserves - **Santiago de Compostela**. It's known mainly for the pilgrimages to the shrine of St James that take place every 25 July, one of Spain's national holidays, celebrated in Compostela with special pomp every 'holy year', when the feast day falls on a Sunday. But the town itself is exceptionally beautiful.

Its central attraction is the Plaza del Obradoiro (also called the Plaza de España), where none of the buildings is less than three hundred years old and most of them go back five hundred or more. The square itself is paved in white stone.

As you enter it from the Calle San Francisco the vast and amazingly complex Cathedral, with its four towers and extensive cloisters, stands on your left. The Bishop's Palace (Palacio Golmírez) adjoins it. You can visit its twelfth century apartments and vast synod hall. Facing you is the College of San Jerónimo, with the fine Town Hall to your right. And behind you is the breathtaking Hostal de los Reyes Católicos, built soon after 1500 by the 'Catholic Monarchs' Ferdinand and Isabella themselves to house pilgrims and today one of the world's loveliest as well as oldest hotels (only the Danieli in Venice, apart from small or very small inns in countries like Britain, Germany, and Denmark, can claim to be older).

The Hostal de los Reyes Católicos is a vast stone structure built around four courts named after the four evangelists. Your room will be 'Mark 18' or 'John 10' or something similar. The furnishings are mostly genuine antiques, and its stone crypt restaurant is almost too splendid to be true. Food, wine, and service live up to the setting.

Exploring the Cathedral and all its treasures needs really to be spread over several days, and you can spend several more merely wandering through the old town and getting to know its tangled streets and many fine buildings. The University is one of them. As in Burgos, the presence of large numbers of very lively youngsters gives the town a feeling almost of perpetual youth - an extraordinary contrast with its late mediæval setting. You'll find the Firestone T20's street plans of Compostela invaluable for finding your way round and identifying places to see.

Yet even all this doesn't exhaust the list of Galicia's lovely towns and striking scenery. **Lugo** and **Orense** stand out. Both are fine towns, set among high rolling hills as you drive eastward from Santiago de Compostela. Lugo, in fact, was once a major halt on the ancient Pilgrims' Road.

If you want to follow any of this track you'll find one of its more southerly branches clearly marked on Firestone's 1:500,000 map of Spain numbered 1. It follows a winding, mountainous side road due east from Compostela to **Puertomarín** and the **Monasterio de Samos** and then to the top of the **Piedrafita Pass** on the modern main road, the NVI, linking Madrid and La Coruña After that it turns southeast to **Ponferrada**, where an iron bridge - hence the name - was built for pilgrims in the tenth century, rather earlier than our own Ironbridge, which claims to be the site of the world's first iron bridge. It continues to **Astorgas**, and then east to León, which we've already seen, and Burgos. This however was only one of several branches. One route, considered specially dangerous for many years, kept close to the coast and passed through Santillana del Mar (see above). East of Burgos, too, there was a choice of routes. One of Europe's oldest guidebooks was intended for the use of pilgrims making for Compostela.

The Basque Lands

We however must go speedily eastwards to the Basque territories, stretching from Bilbao to the Pyrenees and beyond. The Basques are an ancient race, with their own language and their own customs (including music, dances, and games such as *pelota*, played in something resembling an enormous open squash court with extraordinary speed and ferocity). Yet virtually nothing is known about their origins. Their language in particular seems to resemble practically nothing else spoken anywhere, and the only objective clue to possible Basque migrations was provided by a French-Basque journalist during a press trip to Bulgaria.

The Bulgarians had regaled her with a lot of their fine food and were reciting some of their most cherished recipes. But she was usually able to interrupt the recitals and complete each recipe because, as she said, it was always pure Basque. Historians unfortunately virtually never consider the evidence provided by culinary habits. The same applies to folk music, though peoples' attitude to their music and to their food and their ways of preparing it are the most deeply-ingrained of all social habits. The bagpipe the Bulgarians call *gaïda* is known as *gaïta* in Spanish Galicia. Yet a massive recent book on the Celts by a well-known Oxford historian hadn't one word to say about their music, and didn't even mention the bagpipes and the bagpipe music they took everywhere.

The Basques themselves call their language *euskara*. Spain's two specifically Basque provinces are known as *Vizcaya* (capital Bilbao: our Biscay is a corruption of Vizcaya) and Guipúzcoa (capital San Sebastián). One of the Basques' ancient chief cities was **Guernica**, today just a small town on the River Oca a few miles inland from the Ría de Guernica. It was the place where Basque leaders for centuries had assembled under a huge oak - one of its descendants is still there - to consider affairs of state, and one of four places where they swore to respect Basque laws and customs. But it's a new town today. On 26 April 1937 Nazi bombers destroyed the unprotected town on its market day, killing two thousand people in three hours. Picasso's anguished painting, called simply *Guernica*, expresses the horror most of the world felt.

Bilbao is the Basques' modern capital. Though based on an ancient small town that hasn't wholly disappeared, it's a busy, not specially attractive industrial centre and port that's best avoided if you're merely driving through.

The **Basque Coast**, known also in

117

Spanish as the **Cornisa Cantábrica**, extends from here to San Sebastián. It consists of friendly, quiet little resorts stretched along a coast of rocks and crags. **Lequeito**, **Ondárroa**, **Zumaya**, **Guetaria**, and **Zarauz** are its main resorts. Apart from their charming old town centres and fine beaches, the corniche road linking them provides wonderful views. Guetaria can also claim the distinction of having been the birthplace of the man who in fact commanded the first ship to sail round the world. Juan Sabastián Elcano took over when Magellan died and brought his ship successfully home. There's a statue erected in his honour close the village's thirteenth century church.

San Sebastián, the Basques' other main centre, is a splendid place. The modern town flanks a scallop-shaped magnificently sandy beach, aptly called the ***Playa de la Concha*** (Shell Beach), with cliff-lined headlands at either end and the delightful old town tucked away in the lee of the eastern cliffs, looking across the beach to the heights of Monte Igueldo. Most of the modern town dates from the nineteenth century. The bayside promenade is impressive and the town seems to be filled very largely with comfortable-looking houses and well-designed modern offices. Elegance in fact is the overwhelming impression it provides.

Needless to say, it offers excellent hotels and restaurants, with the Monte Igueldo, high on its hill above the town, famous for the clay-pigeon shooting that provides better-off Spaniards with one of their

most appreciated sports. The tiny Old Town makes a delightful contrast, and contains the very impressive 18 July Square (Plaza de 18 de Julio). This is lined with arcades, that have numbered box balconies above them, a relic of the aristocratic seventeenth century *correderas* that were the forerunners of Spain's modern bullfighting traditions.

From San Sebastián to the French frontier at Hendaye it's only twelve miles or so by a fast motorway which comes right through from Bilbao. **Irun**, on Spain's side of the border, has nothing special to offer, but **Fuenterrabía**, on a headland directly north, facing Hendaye Plage, is an attractive seaside village with a pleasant *parador*, converted from an old mansion.

Specifically Basque territories continue inland for some distance and also far into France. The Basques have always regarded themselves as a separate nation, and resent the frontier that splits them into two parts. In bygone days, when communications were slower, they mostly lived their own lives in their own way, but their incorporation into two separate nations was never happy. After the bombing of Guernica and the Civil War even the small degree of independence they then enjoyed was removed. It has now been largely restored with the establishment of Spain's regional parliaments in 1976. But the more fanatical Basques are still far from content.

The Pyrenees

The long line of the **Pyrenees** stretches all the way from the Atlantic to the Mediterranean, rising at Monte Perdido's centrally placed summit to 11,008 feet. At either end however the land is nearly flat - in fact, the frontier beween France and Spain in Basque territory is formed largely by the River Bidassoa. The region used to be famous for its smugglers.

It's better known today for its often magnificent scenery, and for the very picturesque Basque villages, such as St- Jean-Pied-de-Port and many others, in the foothills on the French side. The Spanish side is attractive too. The Pyrenees for much of the time are a very green range - in summer at least. In parts they're covered with woodlands, and in places there are spectacular bursts of wild rock landscapes. Much of the land too is either cultivated or used for pasture until you reach the highest stretches.

A number of passes with altitudes that increase towards the range's central area cross from France into Spain and are all fascinating to drive. The first two, the **Dancharinea** and the **Puerto de Ibañeta**, more usually called the Pass of Roncesvalles from the village on the Spanish side, have roads that lead to **Pamplona**, capital of the former small kingdom of Navarre. Roncesvalles, reached from St-Jean-Pied-de-Port through a long gorge, is famous for the battle described by the epic folk ballad, the *Chanson de Roland*. It tells how a handful of gallant Christians, Roland and twelve peers of Charlemagne's Holy Roman Empire, fought a desperate battle against Moslem hordes in 778.

Pamplona's main claim to modern fame is as the setting of Hemingway's novel *The Sun Also Rises*. It was inspired largely by the 'running of the bulls' that takes place - still - from 6 to 20 July each year, when bulls intended for the evening bullfight run early in the morning through onlookers crowding the palisaded streets on their way to being corralled in the bullring. Pamplona inevitably becomes hopelessly crowded then. But it's also a pleasant town to stay in and explore, especially outside the summer's main heat. The old city's walls on one side occupy a bluff overlooking the River Arga.

The next main pass to the east (there are minor ones between) leads up from the lovely old French town of Oloron-Sainte-Marie to **Candanchu** just inside Spain below the Col de Somport (for some reason the French name seems always to be used). The Col de Somport lies in France's Pyrenees National Park, while Candanchu is a sort of ski resort that went a bit wrong. Its position's perfectly good, and its snow's fine. But it depends mainly on a now half-disused railway line buried under the mountains in a vast tunnel that emerges at the grandiose **Canfranc International Station** miles below Candanchu. The huge building was intended for both French and Spanish use, but it looks very odd today in its lonely glory.

El Formigal below the next pass, the **Col de Portalet**, has taken over as the area's popular ski spot - and very popular it is, too, and very well equipped. **Sallent de Gállego**, well over four thousand feet above sea level, is El Formigal's base town, and the road through it takes you down to the lowland centre of **Jaca**, which lies on the main road running west to east below the Pyrenees as close as any road can. **Berdún**, about twenty miles west, is well-known for its birdwatching. By now we've left the former tiny kingdom of Navarre and the Province of Pamplona that is its modern equivalent and have entered Huesca Province in the ancient Kingdom of Aragón.

The attractive wild valleys and gaunt mountains of the **Ordesa National Park**, reached from **Torla** on the road running up the next valley to the east, occupy an area west of **Monte Perdido**, the Pyrenees' highest point. The region became a National Park in 1918, only months after Covadonga. France's famous **Cirque de Gavarnie**, a great curve of cliff left by receding ice, lies just across the frontier. Limited camping is available in the Ordesa National Park, and you can stay in the hotel at Torla. But the countryside is so wild that you're obliged either to walk (distances are considerable: be warned) or to travel by hired jeep. A high rough track crosses the frontier to the Cirque de Gavarnie. Lots of people find the effort of getting around in this region very worthwhile. It's one of the Pyrenees' loveliest and remotest parts.

A wonderfully placed *parador* on Monte Perdido's further side offers another comfortable place to stay, with the minor ski resort of **Benasque** not far away (if you

happen to be a crow and able to fly in a straight line). Then **Viella** and another useful *parador* in the valley beyond that, on the road running through a long tunnel towards St Bertrand de Comminges in France. Two streams rise on either side of this pass. One is called the Garonne. After linking up with the Lot and the Dordogne it ends up as the vast estuary below Bordeaux. The one on the Spanish side, totally unknown and wholly without distinction, bears the name Garona. Southwest of Viella the **Aigües Tortes National Park** offers superb scenery and a wealth of mountain wildlife. Your exploring base is **Espot**.

One more valley and we've reached the little independent country of **Andorra**, once remote and almost unreachable, today very popular with holidaymakers all year round - the skiing is excellent and so is the mountain walking - as well as being an up-and-coming offshore banking centre and tax haven. It's also a very beautiful place. A fair proportion of its foreign population consists of sensible retired Brits. Andorra has no direct taxes.

Its capital is **Andorra la Vella** and **Encamp** its only other main town. In effect the whole country consists of a single Pyrenean valley. Its joint heads of state are the President of France and the Spanish Bishop of Urgel. The official language is Catalan, but almost everyone speaks French and Spanish as well, and many people add English too. Andorra must be unique in having absolutely no official currency. French and Spanish money circulates freely - and almost anything you care to produce is readily accepted.

By now the Pyrenees' general height is descending. At **Puigcerda**, with Bourg Madame on the frontier's French side, we come to a major Pyrenean road-crossing, though not exactly the easiest in this half of the range. Another popular and well-placed ski resort has grown up in a side valley south of Puigcerda, at **La Molina**, with the ski settlement of **Super Molina** above it.

Now the mountains are clearly descending towards the Med. On their French side the road from Bourg Madame to Perpignan, ancient capital of the Kingdom of Majorca (see Chapter 4) passes through **Prades**, home for many years of the self-exiled Spanish cellist Pablo Casals and famous for the annual festival that he initiated. On the mountains' southern side we're back in Catalan territory, close to where we started our tour of Spain, but more in contact with inland Catalonia than with the coast.

It has been possible to give only the briefest account of the Pyrenees' many delights. It's wonderful territory to drive as well as walk in. But if you take your car, or try to explore the area in a hire car from the Costa Brava, remember that the distances can be enormous. On the Spanish side nearly all the roads run north and south in mountain valleys, and links between them are scarce. Ten miles in a direct line may represent fifty or more by road - and the going is rarely easy.

Inland Catalonia

But what about inland Catalonia?

One or two spots close enough to the coast for easy excursions have been mentioned. There are many others. **Seo de Urgel**, for instance, whose bishop (or more accurately archbishop) is joint head-of-state of Andorra, is a beautifully placed old city with a magnificent twelfth century Cathedral. There's an even earlier church attached to one corner of the Cathedral cloisters.

Ripoll, on the main road from Puigcerda to Barcelona, is another very attractive small Pyrenean-Catalan town. But it's famous chiefly for the former Monastery of Santa Maria, founded in the ninth century in territory that had been devastated by the Moors. Like Cassino in Italy, three centuries older than Ripoll, its library became one of the channels by which the learned works of the ancient world reached still untutored Western Europe. Ripoll's great virtue was that it acted as a vital link between Moslem scholars who had inherited translations of the works of Aristotle and Plato and Galen and others and Europeans to whom they were still unknown.

But Seo de Urgell and Ripoll are only two of many spots worth exploring in Catalonia's interior. If you feel like a really long day's outing (you'll need two drivers), cut across country from your Costa Brava resort to Figueras and from there to Ripoll. Then turn northeast to the very attractive town of **Camprodón**, cross into France at the relatively little used Aras Pass, and join the motorway near Le Boulou for the return journey back to your base via the main frontier crossing at Le Perthus. Or just go as far as **Bañolas**, only twelve miles northwest of Gerona. It's an ancient settlement - and a flourishing modern waterskiing centre, thanks to its vast lake.

Back to Andalucia

We've made a circuit of almost the whole of Spain. It remains only to mention one or two inland towns on its eastern side which, if truth be told, seem to contain little of gripping interest. **Zaragoza**, just off the motorway that links Barcelona with Bilbao right across Spain's interior, has a very impressive town centre backing onto the River Ebro.

It was a major Roman city that became for four centuries the capital of a minor Moslem state. Its name is derived from the Latin Colonia Caesar Augusta via the Arabic Sarakusta, and you can still see bits of the Roman wall close to the Tourist Information Office. Today it's Spain's fifth largest city. Its sightseeing centre is the ***Plaza del Pilar***, which contains the huge church built to house the Virgin of the Pillar, the Town Hall, and the sixteenth century Lonja or

Exchange, where merchants once met to do business. Often referred to as a Cathedral, the church commemorates the Virgin Mary's appearance in front of St James the Apostle himself in 40 AD, leaving an otherwise inexplicable pillar to show she'd been there. The real Cathedral, smaller than Santa Maria del Pilar, lies beyond the Lonja.

But it can't honestly be said that Zaragoza is worth a special journey. Some of the old streets leading off the Plaza del Pilar are pleasant without being specially exciting, and the view you get of Zaragoza's famous towers from the motorway is impressive.

Much the same applies to the other main towns down this side of Spain. **Lérida**, **Teruel**, **Albacete**, **Cuenca**, **Soria**, and the rest have little to attract visitors, though all have places of interest to see if you happen to be driving through or visiting friends.

South of this region we're back in the semi-desert lands of inland Almeria and the mountains of Andalucia.

9.   Land, History and Culture

The land

Spain's landscapes have lots of characteristics we don't much notice in Britain, particularly if we're intent primarily on choosing a good beach. For starters, it's Europe's most mountainous country after Switzerland. The country's bordered by mountains on three of its four sides - and they're much higher than we think.

The Cordillera Cantábrica runs almost the length of its northern coast, not many miles inland, and rises to 8688 feet. The Pyrenees separate Spain from France - and their highest point is over 11,000 feet. Portugal's mountains close Spain in on the west as you quickly discover if you have to drive, say, from Madrid to Lisbon. Andalucia's heights separate sea and central land mass with a range that boasts Spain's highest point, Mulhacén above Trevélez, 11,211 feet above sea level.

More mountains cut across the interior. The Sierra Morena effectively separates southern from central Spain. The Toledo Mountains and the Guadarrama range hem in Madrid on the north, west, and southwest. And the Iberian Cordillera, making an angle with the Pyrenees, cuts pretty well right across northern Spain from the Cordillera Cantábrica to the sea between the River Ebro's mouth and Valencia, with a spur continuing to Cabo de la Nao to give Benidorm and Denia their mountainous hinterland. And as if this weren't enough, the **average** land altitude in Spain is over 2000 feet - rather like everyone living permanently on the summit of a medium-high Lake District mountain.

All this makes life pretty tough for the majority of Spaniards, despite modern life's mod cons - and it was vastly tougher in the past. The **meseta**, as the relatively flat inland areas between the mountains are called, can be bitterly cold in winter and blazing hot in summer. When an inland town shopkeeper greets you before noon with: '¡Ay, que ' calor!' (Heavens! What heat!) reckon on its being appreciably over 100°F before very long, and see that you're safely tucked up for an hour or two's rest in the shade by soon after 2 pm.

If you're working in the fields (which was most people's main occupation till relatively recently), the obvious thing to do is to carry on until the heat begins to be oppressive - a bit after 1 pm - and then to break for lunch and a siesta, followed by another outdoor stint until sundown around 7.30 or 8 pm (there's much less variation in sunset times than in our latitudes), followed by a wash and your evening meal. Spanish midday and evening mealtimes are **very** logical.

The coasts are naturally milder than the interior. The sea sees to that, though along the Costa Brava cold winds from the mountains limit the season to little more than summer. But even this isn't quite the whole basic story. The land below the Pyrenees and between the Cordillera Cantábrica and the sea is sometimes called 'Wet Spain' because of the rain. On the north coast, in particular, a fine drizzle is normal at almost any time of the year, and no one ventures out without a very brightly coloured umbrella unless the weather's obviously set fair. The east coast's southern part, on the other hand, is exceptionally dry, with near-desert erosion common in Almeria Province. Widespread irrigation from vast inland dams has become a feature of modern Spain in many areas apart even from Almeria.

People and history

But what of the people who've lived in these not always hospitable landscapes? The earliest we know anything about were Celtic and Iberian tribes. Phoenicians started establishing coastal trading stations about 1000 BC, and mining Rio Tinto minerals too, exploited even earlier by Mycenean Greeks. They also penetrated inland in places. Greek traders began visiting the coasts around 600 BC (they traditionally considered Gibraltar

and Djebel Musa, the mountain above Ceuta in Morocco, to be the 'Pillars of Hercules', the edge of the world's land-mass, though in fact Greeks had sailed right round Africa before 500 BC).

The Romans came next. Coastal trading posts had had little effect on the mainland tribes - until Rome and Carthage began to fight for supremacy in the Mediterranean. Three bouts of exceptionally bitter warfare ended with Rome's total victory in 146 BC. Their rule lasted six hundred years and left abundant traces. When its final decline resulted in a power vacuum, invading Christian Visigoths took over but only for a century. Remains of Visigoth churches and artefacts have survived in places.

The Visigoths, as well as the original Celtic and Iberian inhabitants, were crushed by the Moorish invasion which began in 711 AD. By 732 the Moors had conquered all Spain and pushed as far north as Poitiers in modern France - only 250 miles from the English Channel. History lessons in Britain never tell us how close we came to being a Moslem country. Nor, incidentally, do they explain the tremendous debt European scholarship owes to Arab and Moorish teachers. Before the great Western universities existed, it was from Moslem (and also Jewish) teachers in places like Córdoba in Spain and Fes in Morocco that the then ignorant Western world rediscovered all the knowledge Greek scientists, doctors, and philosophers could offer.

We've seen a few of the Moslem buildings that still survive in Spain.

Christian architecture began to establish itself only when the Moors were being driven out. The process began with the battle of Covadonga in 722, but wasn't properly under way till the eleventh and twelfth centuries.

Thanks to continuous quarrels between Spain's Christian kings (and also between the Moslem rulers) it was only in the late fifteenth century, when the great kingdoms of Aragón and Castile, which had both already absorbed lesser neighbours, were united under the 'Catholic Monarchs' Ferdinand and Isabella, that the Moors were finally defeated and almost all expelled.

The event coincided with Columbus's discovery of America. Gold and silver poured into Spain fron its New World settlements, and the country's 'Golden Age' began, marked by achievements in the arts and literature as much as by new wealth. It coincided also with increased activity by the Inquisition. Thanks to changing economic conditions and growing laxity in religious establishments, Church reform was in the air. Spain's Lowland territories were fighting back and England refused to be conquered.

The Catholic Establishment reacted fiercely. Jews and Moslems, previously left mostly in peace, were sometimes attacked as intensely as dissenting Christians. Despite the upsurge of Catholic vigour Holland and the Lowlands achieved their freedom in 1609, the year in which the last Moors were also expelled from Spain. But through all these upheavals Catholic Spain remained

firmly, almost aggressively Catholic - and that attitude's still dominant today, despite the modern world's strong contrary influences.

The Golden Age lasted barely a century. The seventeenth, eighteenth, and early nineteenth centuries were filled largely with a series of wars fought in Spain on behalf of royal rulers in various parts of Europe, with England very closely involved (on Spain's side this time against the invading French) in the terrible Peninsular War of the early nineteenth century. Some of our Guards regiments' proudest battle honours date from this period.

By now the economic climate was changing fast. Spain couldn't sidestep the effects of the Industrial Revolution. A new, economically influential non-aristocratic, non-peasant 'middle' class began to grow up. The nineteenth century was taken up largely with political struggles between this new class and the old rulers (the details of all the risings and wars make pretty tedious reading). Spain first became a republic in 1873, but reverted to monarchy a year later.

Along with growing industrialisation yet another section of the population was soon requiring a share of power - the industrial 'working' class. It was largely to fight down their demands that the dreadful Civil War of 1936-39 was fought, with the German and Italian dictators taking the opportunity to try out some of their weapons against the Republicans and the Basques.

General (later 'Generalísimo') Franco had led the Nationalist revolt, and retained control of the country until his death in 1975, taking no part in World War II. Thanks largely to personal interventions by Spain's present King, what started as a rather uneasy parliamentary democracy is now pretty firmly settled, despite residual hankering after an authoritarian restoration by a few disaffected Army officers and the like.

Just as much as invasions by Carthaginians, Romans, Moors and others, these more recent events have marked Spain very strongly. Antagonisms haven't wholly disappeared, but new energy and drive has been pretty obvious since 1975. And new freedom has led to such things as a sudden upsurge of feminist feeling (to say nothing of more aggressive driving). In all sorts of ways Spain's atmosphere has changed - and is still in flux.

Literature and music

We need however to look at some other aspects of the country's life and history. The language - or should one say languages? - that Spain speaks today are directly descended from Latin (apart from Basque, whose origins no one knows). For many centuries Spain has supported outstanding literary works. Even in Roman days several leading late-period authors came from Spain rather than from Rome or Italy. And in subsequent centuries the country has produced more great writers than most people in Britain realise. The musicality of the Spanish language, its delicacy of touch, and its rich imagery make it a wonderfully versatile tool in the hands of an able writer.

In the 'Golden Century' the playwrights Lope de Vega, Tirso de Molina (the first man to celebrate the adventures of Don Juan), and Calderón achieved international fame, as did the novelists Mendoza and Cervantes, author of Don Quixote, almost the only work of Spanish literature that everyone has heard of. But they were not alone. People who talk about the 'picaresque' novel as a distinct art form rarely appreciate that the term derives from the Spanish word *pícaro*, meaning rascal. The world's first racily picaresque novel, by an anonymous author, appeared in Spanish in 1554. And it was at around this time that the mystics St John of the Cross and his friend St Teresa of Ávila were producing their remarkable works. Mysticism may not be to everyone's taste. But the mere sound of St John's poems is pure magic.

In later centuries novelists like Unamuno, essayists such as Ortega y Gasset, and poets such as Ibañez and Jiménez continued this high tradition. In recent years South America has become a main centre of Spanish literature. But the figure of the poet, playwright, musician, and friend of Dali and Buñuel, Federico García Lorca still towers over the scene, even though he was shot by Nationalist fanatics in Granada in 1936, when he was only thirty-seven.

One of Lorca's most interesting qualities was the respect and love he seems to have had for his country's traditional (ie, unwritten but widely known to ordinary people) music and verse. This is an aspect of Spain which, like so much else in the country, is quite inadequately understood and appreciated. If you can get hold of either of the Hispavox LP albums titled *Antologia del Folklore Musical de España* you'll begin to understand a little of what it means. The albums' contents are a very long way from the picture postcard image of Spain's music presented by composers like Ravel, to say nothing of lesser musicians' vulgarisations.

The Hispavox LPs illustrate genuine village music from every corner of the country. Even so, they're only a taste of what Spain can offer. Research for four Radio 4 programmes on *Christmas Around the World* revealed that Spain has not hundreds but thousands of traditional Christmas carols. Many have never been heard outside their own villages. Some are still available only in manuscripts preserved in churches and monasteries. Though usually simple, a large proportion are extremely attractive.

Ninteenth-twentieth century Spanish composers such as Albéniz (1860-1909), Granados (1868-1916), de Falla (1876-1946), and Turina (1881-1948) drew heavily on Spain's vast fund of traditional folk music and even more heavily on the spirit of that music. Earlier composers such as Fernando Sor (1778-1839) and the sixteenth century polyphonist Victoria had kept more strictly to 'high culture' West European forms.

The art of food and wine

Another of Spain's folk arts much appreciated by Spaniards but very little known to outsiders is cooking. Tourist hotels and restaurants serve mostly the now international choice of steaks, pastas (including the ubiquitous spaghetti bolognese), omelettes, chips and so on, with Spain represented by *paellas*, which strictly belong to the country's rice-growing regions around Valencia. If you've Spanish friends who'll take you out to the sort of restaurant they themselves patronise you'll get a very different picture.

The fish dishes of Catalonia (and parts of Andalucia), the northern *fabadas* (spicy bean dishes that can include almost every sort of poultry, meat, and sausage), the *chilindrones* (piquant sauces in which poultry, meat, etc is pot-roasted), the *cocidos* (stews) that vary with every region and almost every cook, and even simple things like freshly-caught fried *boquerones* (fish similar to anchovies) can be pure delight. The most widely appreciated festive dish is roast sucking-pig (*cochinillo asado*), but it belongs, strictly speaking, to Castile.

All these however are more or less everyday eating-out dishes. How about a meal based on fennel soup with bread cubes fried in garlic, followed by kid stewed in almond sauce? It's the sort of simple but perfect meal that you never forget. Unfortunately this sort of thing's becoming rarer and rarer as country people adopt the towns' tastes and habits. But you'll still find it in a few mountain villages if you look and ask and show real interest.

127

For starters (**entremesas**) in regular Spanish restaurants you'll normally get a choice of hams, fish canned in oil (sardines, anchovies, maybe mussels), salad vegetables, green or black olives, a range of shellfish, and possibly hot sweetbreads or kidneys served in tasty sauces. Soups vary from the garlic-and-onion concoctions of Castile to the delicious ice-cold **gazpachos** of Andalucia. Carrot soup can be very tasty too.

Fish is served in all sorts of ways, including many never thought of by ordinary cooks (ever thought of putting ham in your trout?). **Zarzuela de mariscos** (mixed shellfish) is one that is fairly popular. It consists of mixed shellfish lightly fried and then cooked in a slightly peppery wine sauce. Omelettes contain everything from potatoes (the popular 'Spanish omelette') to crabs' tails. Tripe is also served in various ways, and the Spaniards do wonderful things with rabbit.

Cheeses are varied and tasty, with numerous local specialities if you know where to look. Fruit can include quinces and custard-apples as well as everything we know at home, and is usually good. For dessert, many hotel restaurants tend to limit themselves to fruit, ice cream and, occasionally, gateau.

If you hunt around however you can find an exceptional array of sweetmeats directly descended from the sugar confectionery developed by Moorish invaders, who themselves arrived some three centuries before sugar reached Europe. Not only soft and hard nougat and concoctions resembling nougat, but also marzipan (said to have been invented in Toledo during a Christian siege when food was running short), and all sorts of little tarts and cakes made with figs, grapes, honey, and sugar are served. And also some very tasty forms of sweet boiled rice.

As for wines, the Rioja region in the north, and Arganda and Valdepeñas in central Spain are probably the best-known wine-growing regions, apart from Jérez. But every province seems to produce an extraordinary quantity of its own wines. While none qualify as 'great' (to use the real wine-bibbers' technical term), many are decidedly acceptable, especially in the setting of a Spanish meal. If you enjoy wine - experiment. And if you'd like a decent brandy you'll find Spanish products such as Terry, Osborne, Soberano, Larios, Fundador, and the more expensive but by no means pricey Carlos III are well worth trying. Locally distilled whisky and gin aren't bad either. The Scot who taught the Spaniards how to distil whisky drank himself to death on their red wine - or so the Spaniards maintain.

A word about **sangria**. In many places a pretty lethal concoction of wine, fruit juices, and spirits is offered to tourists under the name of **sangria**, especially when groups have a 'welcome' drink at their hotels and so on. The real stuff is made without spirits, and is a very pleasant cold thirst-quenching drink that includes some wine.

If you want to avoid alcohol altogether bottled spa waters are always available. The most popular is Lanjarón, from the town near Granada. Other brands include

Aralar, Insalus, Vichy Catalán, and others. Malvella is a bit fizzy in a special way. You can have your Lanjarón with or without gas. The waiters always ask: '¿Con gas o sin gas?'

The visual arts

But what of Spain's more visual arts? The country's painters seem to have received almost as little attention as its authors from Britain's public.

Three great schools of painting emerged during the sixteenth century at Valencia, Seville, and Madrid. Francisco Ribalta (1551-1628) and José de Ribera (1568-1656) were Valencia's leading artists. Seville boasted Morales (1509-1586), Zurbarán (1598-1663), Velasquez (1599-1660), and Murillo (1618-1682). Madrid's outstanding name was the court artist El Greco (1548-1682), with Francisco Goya coming later (1746-1828). Spain's most valuable art collection is the Museo del Prado in Madrid. But you can see works by many of these artists elsewhere too.

More recent artists such as Utrillo, Dali, Miró, and Picasso have continued their predecessors' tradition, and are better known than most of the earlier painters are.

Spain's architecture is, again, relatively little known but very striking. We've looked at various buildings dating from the period of Moorish domination. Distinguishing the different periods of Moorish building and its colourful decorations isn't easy. It would need too many illustrations to handle it effectively here. Basically, simplicity

gave way to ever greater complexity.

One interesting result of Moorish rule was the mixing of Moorish and Christian outlooks in the so-called mozarab and mudejar styles. The term mozarab is applied to work by Christians done for Moorish masters. Mudejar describes the products of Moors working in Christian territory and on Christian themes. Trying to describe the differences briefly in words is virtually impossible. When you see it you begin to appreciate the differences.

Of the straightforward architectural styles - Romanesque, Gothic, and so on - Spain has few Romanesque churches or monasteries outside Catalonia and the north (notably along the Pilgrim Road to Compostela: also Valladolid's Old Cathedral), mainly because the Moors ruled the rest of the country in the years when Romanesque was the accepted building style.

In the fourteenth and fifteenth centuries Gothic took over and developed specifically Spanish forms during the reign of the 'Catholic Monarch' Isabella of Castile (1474-1504). Lace-like carving, heraldic motifs, and other imaginative decoration began to cover whole facades of civil as well as religious buildings. By the early years of the sixteenth century these 'Isabelline' fantasies had developed into the even richer 'plateresque' style, in which the carvings clearly resembled the relief work of silversmiths. Salamanca University's famous entrance gate is one of the best examples of plateresque. But it's not alone.

The vast El Escorial monastery-palace outside Madrid, commissioned by Philip II in 1557, is a sort of determined reaction against this tendency to rich - maybe over-rich - decoration. In a way it's a magnificent monument to austerity, overpowering and a little repellent because of its monastic sternness, yet attractive at the same time because of its majestic proportions. In some ways it's a disturbing building.

The clash between austerity and ornateness continued into the Baroque period, both movements fuelled perhaps by religious fervour. José Churriguera (1665-1725) who designed the altarpiece of St Stephen's Monastery in Salamanca gave his name to the specially ornate form of Baroque known as 'chirrigueresque'.

Of more recent work the best known by far is the Church of the Holy Family (Sagrada Familia) in Barcelona. It was designed and built in idiosyncratically fantastic forms by the extraordinary architect Antonio Gaudí, inspired to some extent by *art nouveau* ideals. Construction was interrupted by the First World War, and wasn't completed when Gaudí died in 1926. A restart was made in the 1940s.

A word should be said about Spanish handicrafts. You'll find a lot of painted pottery on sale at many resorts, along with basketwork of various sorts, a fair amount of leatherwork, and sometimes ceramic tiles. Most modern wares however can hardly compete with older work, such as the wrought-iron balconies and grilles and pottery and tiles that formed part of many older houses and households.

Customs and character

But how does this background affect ordinary Spaniards? And where does bullfighting fit in? (The British seem much more obsessed with bullfighting than most modern Spaniards are.) It's not too difficult to detect a strand of unity in everything that makes up Spain.

Countryside and landscapes are vastly harsher than any but the wildest parts of Britain. And the climate is enormously less easy-going and hospitable than you'd imagine from a couple of weeks on some sunny coast. The Spaniards are a very tough nation. When the Civil War was forced on them mainly by their historical and economic development they fought it with all the ferocity they'd shown in all their wars against foreigners on their own soil in previous centuries.

They're an extremely proud people. By 'proud' I don't mean snooty. They don't look down on other people. But they're not going to let anyone look down on them either. Almost every summer some Brit, or maybe a group of them, gets himself arrested and possibly jailed for making derogatory remarks about Spain or for being disrespectful to the Spanish flag or the like. Looking at Spain's history and thinking of the number of punishing wars that have taken place on their territory in one century after another - something Britain hasn't known for a thousand years - this self-defensive pride can hardly be considered surprising.

Most nations anyway respond far more sharply to national insults than Brits do.

But aren't bullfights needlessly cruel? More so than, say, foxhunting or deer stalking? One of the things most Brits don't understand is the amount of skill and ritual that goes into bullfighting. It resembles foxhunting in many ways - it certainly requires a huge amount of skill and a great deal of training - especially for the matador, the team leader who actually makes the kill. Today however, even in towns like Córdoba, where great bullfighters used to be treated almost as gods, interest in the sport has declined. Footballers occupy a far higher position in most people's eyes.

If you travel through Spain and deal with the people you meet, maybe in towns and maybe in out-of-the-way places, you'll find them extremely friendly and hospitable, and also extremely courteous, especially if you treat them in the same way. Indeed, they can often behave in a positively courtly way. And that's a characteristic that our ancestors repeatedly commented on as long ago as the days of the first Queen Elizabeth.

Do remember little points like these when you're dealing with your Spanish hosts. Don't judge them as though they were fellow-Brits, and above all don't treat Spain as though it belongs to you. Try always to be courteously, almost studiously polite. That's considered normal. Brusque and abrupt expressions of irritation and the like, such as we use when we think someone's being unhelpful or stupid, seem just needlessly rude in Spain.

And remember how hurt Spaniards may feel should one of their own number be discourteous to you. Should you, for instance, have to report to the police a theft or maybe just the fact that someone has rammed your car while you weren't in it, you may feel that the police start by seeming unfriendly. If you watch carefully, though, you'll realise that they're basically just very embarrassed that any Spaniard should be so unfriendly to a stranger, and they're ashamed for their country. You have to keep assuring them, maybe for quite some time, that this could happen anywhere - even in London or wherever it is you live.

If things do go wrong - and I sincerely hope they won't - do try, whatever else you do, to keep your temper and remain studiously courteous yourself. Don't add to your hosts' embarrassment. And above all, don't force them into feeling you're too difficult anyway to deal with. This isn't perhaps the normal British attitude. But when in Spain. . . .

One way things may go wrong is if you travel to some remote (and cheap) village. Your way of life, the way you spend your money, your behaviour, even your clothes can easily strike local people as odd and therefore undesirable. Country people are extremely conservative in Spain as elsewhere. No one in such circumstances will be impolite. But they may not show themselves particularly friendly. Unless, of course, you go out of your way to show special friendliness and make a real attempt to understand their ways of seeing things. You can do a tremendous amount with signs and smiles even if you speak no Spanish.

Tourism today

Finally, a few words about modern tourism and its development in Spain. It's something we've all benefited from, and hope to go on enjoying for a very long time, yet it's something almost everyone takes for granted. Practically no one gives the Spaniards the credit they undoubtedly deserve for the huge amount of work they've done in very carefully nurturing developments that could so easily have gone very wrong indeed.

The story of how Spain was launched on its meteoric postwar tourism career seems never to have been told. In 1953, when the British were far and away Europe's most numerous travellers, Thos Cook & Son's Publicity Manager, Bill Cormack, put out a press release saying it was perfectly possible to have a good holiday on the Costa Brava on the £25-worth of foreign currency which was all that was then allowed. You could use sterling to pay your fare to any part of the world, but your hotel bill and all your spending money had to come out of the £25.

British journalists, of course, moaned continuously about this £25 allowance - moaning's their main occupation. The immediate response to Cook's press release was a phone call from Fanny Craddock telling Bill Cormack he was talking rubbish. His response was to send Fanny and her husband

down - by train, of course - for a holiday in Tamariú at Thos Cook's expense.

The result was a glowing article on the delights of the Costa Brava and how well you could manage there on the £25 allowance. Thos Cook's bookings rocketed. Other tour operators moved in, and foreign holiday companies followed suit.

Packages with air travel started two years later, and all Europe's travel industry, led by Britain, began looking at other parts of Spain. In 1956 a tiny fishing village in the country's southern part was 'discovered'. It had only three tiny hotels, but there were enough rooms to cope with tourists brought by 36-seater DC3s. And that was how Torremolinos started its tourism career. In the early days you had to fly to Gibraltar. There was no airport at Málaga for quite a time.

As everyone knows, Spain has never looked back since then. What everyone does not know, and what is never mentioned, even by travel journalists who ought to know better, is that the bulk of Spain's success in this far from easy field has been and still is due to careful government management.

In the mid-fifties the Mediterranean's two leading holiday countries were - not to put too fine a point on it - making a mess of their tourism. Standards were low, overcharging was rife, and a lot of visitors went away far from satisfied. The Spaniards learnt from this long before the countries who were letting themselves down did. They introduced all sorts of controls on prices, and all sorts of incentives for maintaining good standards - and they made everyone working in Spanish tourism toe the line.

If you talk to anyone involved in Spain's holiday businesses you'll soon discover how rigorously standards are imposed. Almost anyone offering public services - hotels, restaurants, railway stations, even roadside petrol stations - still has to maintain a Complaints Book for public use, and it's inspected every month. Maximum prices in restaurants and hotels depend strictly on gradings, which are decided by the national and provincial authorities. And so on. It's a great pity that the British press, which gives so much publicity to the occasional hiccup resulting from over-booking or from over-optimistic fixing of completion dates for new hotels (which good British tour operators are well aware of, and try to deal with before their clients arrive), never mentions the achievements of the Spanish authorities. The public understands better and votes with its feet and its purse.

We also hear a lot of ill-informed sneers at the 'Costas'. But no journalist ever seems to mention that these are in effect brandnames very sensibly invented to encourage group publicity for all the resorts of a province or pair of provinces. Too many people, regrettably, seem unaware of this fact. Mistakes are inevitably made. Everything in the garden isn't always lovely all the time. But the Spaniards, as well as the country they live in, surely deserve to be given credit for what they've achieved and are still achieving.

133

10. Useful Information

Before you leave

(This section is intended primarily for first-time travellers. But others may find it useful too.)

You need to do three things before you set out. First, you must obtain a valid 'travel document' of some sort. Second, you must take out insurance against loss of deposits should you be prevented at the last moment from travelling because of your own or a close relative's illness, or be faced with heavy unscheduled expenses during the trip (you don't **have** to do this, but it's silly not to). And, third (obviously), you have to make your bookings.

Getting a travel document and insuring against loss of deposits has been put **before** making your booking. There's no point in booking if you can't travel because you've no sort of valid passport. And insurers won't pay for lost deposits if you insure **after** the booking is made. Making it **at the same time** as the booking is the simplest solution, provided you're happy with the insurance you're offered.

Both the British Visitor's Passport, valid for one year, which you buy over the counter at any main post office for £7.50, and the full British Passport, costing £15.00, which lasts for ten years, can be used for travel to and in Spain without further

formality. You obtain the latter by post from various Passport Offices scattered round the UK or, in cases of special rush, over the counter.

Application forms for both types of passport are available at all main post offices, and spell out very clearly what you need in the way of photographs and proofs of identity. If you and both your parents were born in the UK, and if you're permanently domiciled there you should have no problems getting your 'travel document'. If you or your father were born abroad, or if you're a woman married to someone born abroad and not a British passport holder, or aren't continuously domiciled in the UK, for heaven's sake apply months before you intend to travel. All sorts of people have had terrible battles over passports, in some cases even after having held a British passport since early childhood.

EEC nationals, including British, and American and Canadian citizens do not need visas for a stay in Spain of up to three months. Citizens of other countries, and anyone thinking of staying longer, should ask for information from any Spanish National Tourist Office or diplomatic mission.

As for insurance, it's as well to take

134

out cover for everything that can possibly go wrong during your trip - loss of deposits, airport delays , baggage theft, illness or accident, and everything else. Schemes where the insurers (not you) make all the on-the-spot arrangements and look after payments have considerable advantages. Good tour operators however will also help and advance you cash in emergencies, especially if you're properly insured.

Think about all this before you make your actual booking and make certain you're insured for deposit loss by the time you pay over the deposits.

Try too to make certain that the holiday you're buying really fits your particular needs. Good travel agents and tour operators are prepared at least to try to answer all the questions you can throw at them. So - if you want to be *certain* that baby-sitters will be on hand, or that you can hire scooters easily, or that there's a good selection of discos, or of excursions, or anything else, badger your travel agent to get answers from the tour operator. And don't be put off with answers that aren't precise and clear.

Stock up before you leave with all the personal toiletries, cosmetics, suntan lotions, sunglasses, tummy upset cures, motion sickness pills, films, babyfoods, baby's nappies, and everything else you're even vaguely likely to need during your trip.

Don't rely on finding anything at your resort. Everything may in fact be there. But looking for stuff after arrival can also waste huge amounts of time. And it may be pricey. If you might hire a car or a scooter, think about buying the appropriate Firestone T map or maps in advance. They're obtainable from Edward Stanford Ltd, 12 Long Acre, London W.C.2.

Modern EEC-style British driving licences are legally valid in Spain, but police in the more out-of-the-way places may not yet be accustomed to dealing with them - and that can waste time, if nothing else. The easiest alternative is an international driving permit provided by the AA or RAC, either by post or over the counter, on production of your current driving licence and a couple of passport-sized photographs. You can also use a Spanish translation of a non-EEC-style driving licence, authenticated by the Spanish Consulate at 20 Draycott Place, London S.W.3.

As for your money, it's easiest to take it all in the form of traveller's cheques, with enough sterling cash to cover your travel to and from the UK airport. You can always change traveller's cheques at your arrival airport (but don't forget to do so). The great advantage of traveller's cheques is that you can get an immediate refund if they're lost or stolen.

Finally, do make sure your home's properly locked up and no telltale signs of your absence left around, like milk bottles or newspapers piling up on the doorstep. If possible, get someone to go in fairly frequently and preserve the place's occupied look.

After you arrive

Money We'll stay with this rather important topic. Spain's currency is the **peseta** (abbreviated pta). Coins include a brass 1 pta, and nickel 5. 25, 50 and 100 ptas. Banknote values are 100, 500, 1000, 2000 and 5000 ptas.

You can take into Spain without formality as much money as you wish in non-Spanish currencies or traveller's cheques. Also any amount of Spanish currency in peseta notes. But you mustn't take out more than 100,000 ptas (around £500) in Spanish currency, nor foreign currency with a value over 500,000 ptas unless you can prove you brought it into Spain.

Eurocheques are widely accepted, and you can use bank cards to draw money from corresponding Spanish banks (get details from your own branch). National Girobank Postcheques allow depositors to withdraw money from Spanish post offices. Many shops, travel firms, and the like accept credit cards.

When changing traveller's cheques or sterling notes go, if possible, to a special exchange office (**cambio**) run by a bank, not one operated by a travel firm or hotel. You usually get better rates from banks. Avoid ordinary bank branches however. Everything seems to take hours there.

Whatever you do, don't carry your passport and traveller's cheques in the same handbag or pocket. You have to produce your passport to cash cheques. But it isn't always too carefully looked at. If someone else has your passport as well as your traveller's cheques, it's relatively easy for him or her to cash them.

Information on arrival Your tour operator's rep will normally give you all the basic information you need. You'll find that many reps, British as well as Spanish, have a remarkably detailed knowledge of the whole area around the resort or resorts they look after. If they can't answer your questions, go to a Tourist Information Office (**Oficina de Turismo**). English will almost certainly be spoken there - it's all Europe's lingua franca today, as well as your native tongue. If it isn't you'll have picked an extremely remote spot! Remember however that they tend to keep shop opening hours (see Other points - Opening times, below). ·

Getting around by public transport

Trains were mentioned several times in describing Costa Dorada resorts near Barcelona. Fares are reasonable and the trains adequately comfortable. Your rep will probably have a good idea of train timings. For longer journeys there are usually expresses available, with supplements payable. You get lower fares on certain days of the week - and pay extra on peak days. Go-as-you-please tickets valid eight or fifteen days, and 'kilometric tickets' valid for specific quantities of travel can also be bought. If you hold both BR **and** Rail Europ Senior Citizen cards (available from BR) substantial reductions are available. The local **Turismo**, as people call it, can usually give you relevant details. But for preference consult the Spanish National Tourist Office before departure.

Long-distance coaches operate between towns, but you may have to hunt around a little to find information. Start at the *Turismo*. If you're sent to pursue your enquiries at a bus station don't be shy about expecting them to find someone who speaks English if you've no Spanish.

Local bus services are usually good where there's a demand for them (eg, up and down between the various segments of Torremolinos and also between Blanes and nearby resorts at the Costa Brava's southern end). But don't rely too readily on buses going exactly where you want. They run to suit local people's working needs and times - not holidaymakers' whims.

Taxis, on the other hand, are inexpensive and with three or four people sharing make even longish journeys seem quite cheap. Prices vary a little from place to place. Consult your hotel receptionist, who will usually know the approximate charge to all the places that tourists normally visit. If you decide to hire a taxi for a longer time - an all-day or half-day excursion to some place of interest, for example - ask the driver what he'll charge and agree the price clearly in advance. A tip of ten per-cent of the taxi fare is usual. Fares are normally displayed on a meter.

Getting around with your own conveyance

One traditional feature of Spanish resorts is the possibility in many places of hiring **scooters** and **mopeds** and, in some spots, **bicycles** as well as **cars**. For a scooter you have to be over 18 and hold a valid (full) driving licence. For a moped you need only be over sixteen (no licence). Bicycles are used a lot in spots that are reasonably flat and are sometimes very useful. Prices, including those for cars, are quite low.

If you hire a car, think seriously about adding collision damage waiver to your bill. Should you have an accident, it avoids, at the very least, worry over what you may have to pay and, at the worst, the possibility of long and perhaps expensive legal arguments. Using a credit card to pay for car hire obviates the need to put down a cash deposit. Very often too you can book a car at the same time as you book your holiday. The special advantages of doing this are that you may get specially negotiated rates and will be certain of a car being available even at the season's height.

Driving laws

It's usually said, perhaps a little glibly, that Spain observes the international driving code. Spain's Highway Code is in fact rather different from ours. No one will be terribly upset if you observe the same rules as in Britain - until you have, or cause, an accident. It's better to know more exactly how you're expected to drive.

Speed limits are 130 km (roughly 83 miles) per hour on motorways and 100 km (62 miles) on other open roads, unless otherwise signposted. In built-up areas the limits vary between 40 and 60 km per hour (25 to 38 mph), but are clearly indicated. Reckon 8 km = 5 miles.

Overtaking You drive on the right, of course, and overtake on the left. Legally, you're expected to give notice of your intention to overtake. Using your indicator lights well before you pull out is normal (hooting is discouraged). Further, when being overtaken you are supposed to let the driver behind you know that it's safe for him to come past by flashing your inside light if it is and your outer one if it's not. Because of the possibility of being accused in court (if there's an accident) of having given misleading indications, some drivers avoid giving any sort of 'come past' signal. This can leave you with the choice of going past when you've not been told the road is clear, or of staying on some slow vehicle's tail.

Truck drivers, luckily, are pretty conscientious about helping other motorists. It's usually only large trucks which seriously obstruct your view ahead, and you come to depend on their drivers' help. One helpful factor on main roads is that the places where overtaking is forbidden are always very clearly marked, not only by solid white lines but also by no-overtaking signs. But Spanish drivers will appreciate your helping them to get by when the road is clear. Flashing your inside indicator as a 'come by' signal is used in a lot of European countries, but understood by very few Brits, it seems.

Priority At intersections of equal-

importance roads you must give way to vehicles on your right. *This includes roundabouts* - which means that anyone joining a roundabout has priority over anyone already on it. Remember however that other non-Spanish drivers of hire cars may be as unaware of this law as you are. Most busier junctions have CEDA EL PASO (stop) or STOP signs with inverted red triangles at appropriate points, but you can't always see these from the priority roads.

Parking This is subject to somewhat complex regulations. In addition to normal safety and obstruction considerations you must park only on the road's near side (the righthand side), except in one-way streets, where you park alongside houses with even numbers on even dates and vice versa. In certain towns, however, you change over parking sides on the 16th of the month. This is indicated by signs. You must not park within 5m (16 ft) of corners, junctions and entrances to public buildings (post offices, police stations, town halls, etc). Nor within 7m (22 ft) of tram and bus stops. In one-way streets you must park only where there's room for two vehicles to drive abreast of your car.

A Blue Zone (*Zona Azul*) operates in some town centres. Here, except between 21.00 and 08.00 (when there is no time limit) you may not park for more than 1½ hours at a time. When doing this you must use a parking disc, obtainable at hotels, travel agents, and town halls. Wrongly parked cars may be towed away. *Note particularly* that parked cars must always be locked.

If you are unavoidably stationary on a main road or motorway you must place a red warning triangle at least 30m (roughly 100 feet) behind your vehicle. Every hire car will normally be provided with one. But check.

Turns The three-point turns beloved of British driving tests are forbidden in Spanish towns. So is reversing into side streets to change direction (in theory at least: some towns' parking arrangements in fact make it necessary to reverse into busy main roads, and many drivers seem not to bother where or how they reverse).

Lights Sidelights only (not even dipped headlights) must be used in built-up areas after dusk. All your lights must at all times be in full working order. You are also legally obliged to carry spare bulbs so that immediate replacements can be made if necessary. Hire firms look after this.

Seat belts These must be worn in front seats.

Traffic penalties and appeals For standard offences such as wrong parking or exceeding the speed limit you are subject to fixed penalties. In towns these are fairly small. On the open road they may be ten times as high. Non-residents have to pay immediately (for which a standard 20% reduction is granted), and have the right of appeal within fifteen days to the provincial capital's *Jefatura de Tráfico* for open-road offences (instructions in English are given on the back of the receipt) and to the local town hall for town offences.

Driving licence This must be carried with you at all times (you can't produce it later at a police station).

Getting away with minor offences In major resorts, where non-Spaniards greatly outnumber Spaniards, police are usually fairly lenient about minor infringements. But don't rely on this if you venture outside the resort area. It's a normal courtesy anyway to respect local laws and customs. And it costs you nothing.

Further points to note when driving include:

'Change of direction' On main roads an ingenious way of avoiding accidents arising from cars having to turn left in front of oncoming traffic is frequent. Slip roads bearing off right have been built which not only allow you to turn right - they also allow you to swing round to the left and cross the road you were on at right angles. You're warned that a slip road of this sort is coming up by the sign CAMBIO DE DIRECCIÓN (change of direction).

Roads Spain's roads have been virtually rebuilt over the past twenty years and are now almost invariably very good. Motorways have numbers prefixed by A (for *Autopista*) and ordinary main roads numbers prefixed by N (for *Nacional*). Roman numerals are sometimes (but not always) used for the major main roads radiating from Madrid. You pay tolls on motorways, but rates aren't high.

Signposting Main destinations on ordinary highways are usually clearly signposted. On motorways, unfortunately, the road's number, which can be near-meaningless, is often given more prominence than destinations. In towns signs often seem to be deliberately placed so low that they can be obscured by everyone and everything including policemen standing and chatting with friends. They don't anyway come up to Britain's usually extremely high standard.

Other road signs   Warning signs that may appear only in Spanish include: CEDA EL PASO (give way: stop); DESVIO (diversion); ESTACIONAMIENTO DE AUTOMÓVILES, often abbreviated PARKING, (car park); PASO PROHIBIDO (no thoroughfare); DIRECCIÓN UNICA (one-way street); ESTACIONAMIENTO PROHIBIDO (parking prohibited); OBRAS (roadworks); PELIGRO (danger). RONDA indicates an urban ringway, CIRCONVALLACIÓN a bypass.

Petrol stations   These are frequent. Virtually all stock 'super' (96-octane), but 'extra' (98-octane) can't be guaranteed everywhere. All petrol stations are legally obliged to keep complaints books in which the public can enter comments (see Other points - Complaints, below). They must also provide ladies' and men's toilets and keep them clean and in good working order. You don't have to be buying petrol or anything else to use them.

Traffic lights   These tend sometimes to be suspended rather high above the road and aren't always easy to see in time. However, flashing yellow lights, usually some two hundred yards in advance of the traffic lights proper, may warn you of their imminence. A flashing red light means 'stop' (not, as in

many other places, 'proceed with caution'). It's often used at places such as level crossings when a train is approaching.

Eating and drinking

If you eat in your hotel or in nearby **restaurants** that cater specifically for tourists you'll find everything very much as at home - but not in less tourist-frequented spots. Like hotels, restaurants are officially inspected and graded into five categories, denoted by one to five forks. It's not unusual for a hotel and its restaurant to be in different categories. Except in hotels however restaurants do not always display their gradings very prominently, although these affect the prices they're allowed to charge.

All prices must by law be publicly displayed, and all restaurants are obliged to provide a set-price meal which includes wine and is called *menú del día*. Another Spanish restaurant speciality is the *platos combinados* ('combined dishes'). This is a sort of smaller set meal. It consists of a reasonably substantial main dish combined with, say, soup, bread, and coffee.

You'll see plenty of **cafeterias** in the larger towns. The word however doesn't mean quite the same as in Britain. Most Spanish cafeterias are in reality small restaurants where you can also get a quick-service (but not necessarily cheaper or simpler) meal by sitting up at the bar. Don't expect them to be cheaper than restaurants. Some are relatively expensive.

Meal times in resorts will be what

you would expect at home. Elsewhere lunch, if intended for Spaniards, is **never** served before 1.30 p.m. and any Spaniard who shows interest in starting his evening meal before 9 p.m. is considered distinctly peculiar if not actually off his rocker. 10 p.m. is quite a normal starting-time.

Bars These abound everywhere, in a vast variety of forms, and are considerd a very normal part of life. One of Granada's best-stocked and best-run bars, for instance, is located beside the main reception desk in a major hospital. It's the obvious and very convenient meeting-place for visitors and patients able to walk.

Bars serve every sort of drink, including coffee, tea, and soft drinks, and usually small snacks and sandwiches as well. A small charge is made for each of the **tapas** (plates of olives, nuts, shrimps, sliced sausage, and other delicacies left on your table or the bar). Don't imagine they're free.

Except in resorts and sophisticated town areas it's still not really normal for women to go into bars alone - despite increasing feminism in Spain. Catholic influence is still dominant.

It is however perfectly normal for **everyone** to go into a bar to use the loos (**servicios**) without being expected to buy a drink. The smarter and more expensive the bar the better the loos are likely to be. If there's an attendant put a few small coins in the saucer. If not, leave a small tip on the bar. And thank the barperson.

Sports and entertainments

If you want to play **tennis** or serious **golf** or enjoy any other sort of sport such as, say, **riding** (which is fairly plentifully provided in Spanish resorts), make sure your travel agent discovers from the tour operator whether it's available at your chosen resort and whether there are any snags (eg, you need a long taxi ride to get to the sports ground or stables). If you're travelling on your own put your questions to the Spanish National Tourist Office in London.

Windsurfing is possible in lots of places - and you can get lessons on hired equipment fairly easily. **Water-skiing** is provided in season in the more sheltered spots (but if it's important to you, ask in advance). Pedalos exist almost everywhere. And in some places **sailing dinghies** are also available. **Scuba diving** is best planned through your home club, though you may use a package tour for your stay at your Spanish base.

As for **evening entertainments**, you can take it that every resort will provide at least some sort of bar or nightspot for relaxation and usually dancing - even if it's only modest canned music. This book's main text tries to indicate where evenings may be specially quiet. In most resorts they're not - or needn't be if you look around.

You'll find that 'folklore' **performances** are also organised for tourists. These, unfortunately, usually offer what the organisers think the tourists want - a lot of noise and colour and action, and not necessarily much of Spain's genuine folk music and dance. Local festivals which at the very least cater as much for residents as for visitors and are often genuinely local events will give you a better idea of the real thing.

In Andalucia a few bars and other venues still act as performing bases for genuine **flamenco** and **cante hondo** artistes. But you have to find a local person to tell you where they are and, usually, to take you along. Strangers with no knowledge of the very complex musical forms aren't very welcome - unless, of course, they show genuine interest and willingness to learn. The drunken lout who thinks it funny to shout '¡Olé!' whenever he feels like it is not the sort of person serious performers appreciate.

In Catalonia you may well find local **cobla** groups, possibly including some traditional local instruments, performing their stately **sardanas** in town and village squares in the cool of the evening. If you're interested, enquire about these and about local festivals from local people whom you meet.

Other points

Children Tour operators' brochures make clear the reductions offered for children of various ages, and the facilities (such as babysitting) available at each resort. In general, you will find that hotels and restaurants take very good care of youngsters. Internationally-known baby foods, such as Heinz and Gerber, are usually available in larger towns

and resorts. But it's better to take your own and travel with certainty rather than just hopefully.

Complaints Under Spanish law every railway station, restaurant, petrol station, and hotel is obliged to keep an Official Complaints Book (**Libro Oficial de Reclamaciones**) and to make it available on request. Should the book not be forthcoming, send your complaint to the Ministry of Information and Tourism's office in the relevant provincial or regional capital (addresses are available from the Spanish National Tourist Office in London). The standards of all establishments obliged to maintain Complaints Books are laid down by law, and the books are regularly inspected. This is just one of the many ways in which careful government management has ensured high quality for Spain's tourism through thirty years of rapid development.

Your travel firm's rep will usually be able to sort out most problems on the spot. If you have to object to something that the tour operator himself is responsible for (inaccurate brochure descriptions, failure to provide facilities you've paid for, or the like), take your complaint promptly and quietly to the rep. If it's not immediately corrected repeat the complaint in writing **and keep an exact copy**. If there's still no action write to the tour operator as soon as you get home, consult your travel agent, and if necessary your solicitor. ABTA (the Association of British Travel Agents) can help achieve a reasonably amicable settlement. Unfortunately, claiming rebates for 'ruined' holidays has become something of a profession nowadays. So, if you've what you consider a genuine complaint, make certain you've all the evidence (copies of letters written, bills paid for extras, photographs if relevant, etc) to support your claim.

Correspondence If people at home are likely to need to contact you while you're away, find out in advance from your travel agent/tour operator how they can best do this and give them the necessary addresses, phone and telex numbers, etc. If you're moving around letters can be sent to any Spanish Post Office for you to collect there. Have them sent to you *under your name as entered in your passport* (which won't necessarily carry the first name your friends address you by) at *Lista de Correos*, followed by the name of the town or village *and its province*. When you go to collect mail at a Post Office you *must* take your passport. There may be a small charge. Allow eight to ten days for letters to reach you.

Dry cleaning Consult your hotel's reception desk.

Electricity 220 or 225 volts, 50 cycles in all main resorts. This means that hair dryers, travelling irons and the like will function as in Britain. You will however need a 'Continental'-type two-pin plug. Adaptors can be bought in electrical equipment shops, from travel agents, etc.

Emergencies and disasters Tour operators' reps, hotel concierges, campsite and hostel wardens, and everyone else dealing regularly with visitors know what to do and will help. Report losses and thefts of property promptly to the police of the locality in which they occurred and obtain from them a certificate confirming your report. If you make a claim on your insurance the company will insist on having this document.

For the same reason keep carefully all receipts for payments made because of illness or accident or the need to return home suddenly (which can be a bit of a nuisance when you're perhaps not exactly fit and you and your family are worried stiff). Good tour operators' reps will normally, of course, do all they can to help.

For other problems (if you lose your passport or are arrested, for instance) contact the nearest British consular representative. Tour operators' reps, hotels, the police, etc will have the address. Beyond providing a temporary travel document to get you back home, diplomatic staff can do no more than supply you with a ticket home by the cheapest route (against a written undertaking to refund the money promptly on your return). They can however provide advice; recommend lawyers, etc.

Credit cards and on-the-spot traveller's cheque refunds nowadays cover most problems that arise from having all your money stolen. But do find out before you leave how you can use your cards in Spain. Above all, keep the little instruction sheet telling you how to claim immediate replacement of stolen or lost traveller's cheques and the record of your cheques' numbers separate from the cheques themselves.

Language You'll not need to use anything but English in the ordinary resorts. However, your use of the basic Spanish courtesies (good morning, thank you, excuse me, goodbye, and the like) when you're dealing with non-English-speakers (maybe through someone who's interpreting) will always be tremendously appreciated. Essential phrases are given in the next chapter's Language Guide.

Laundry Take some detergent and do your own for preference. If you need something washed more carefully than you can manage in your hotel room ask hotel reception how to get it done. The chambermaids usually look after things and wash and iron very well. You pay them separately.

Lavatories Public lavatories as we know them are pretty rare and it's perfectly normal to use those in bars, as already explained. The essential words are: *servicios* (lavatories), *señores* or *caballeros* (gentlemen), and *señoras* (ladies). Most use pictorial signs as well.

Opening times (shops, banks, museum, etc, not the bars: they stay open all day and sometimes well into the night) Town shops mostly open from 09.00 to about 13.00 or 13.30 and from 16.00 to 19.30 or later. They close on Sundays, national holidays, and for some major local festivals. Resort shops catering specially for visitors may keep much longer hours and open on Sundays as well. But don't bank on it. Markets begin at 06.00 and are at their busiest around 09.00, beginning to close by 12.00 or earlier. Banks open 09.00-14.00 Monday to Friday and 09.00-13.00

on Saturday. Their special exchange office *cambios* keep shop hours and in resorts may stay open a lot longer.

Museum opening times are much more complex and variable. The general tendency is to open between 09.00 and 10.00 and close between 13.30 and 14.00, with a possible further two or three hours from 16.00. Closing day is normally Monday (all day) and possibly Saturday or Sunday afternoon. A few very major museums and galleries, notably the Prado in Madrid, stay open right through the day. But this is unusual. Don't reckon on other places you want to visit being open between 13.30 (at the latest) and 16.00. Sensible people don't move around then anyway. And they rest after strenuous weekends on Mondays.

Postal services Letterboxes are painted yellow. You buy stamps from your hotel reception desk, from kiosks selling postcards and souvenirs, from tobacconists (whose red cigar sign indicates that they sell also stamps) and, in case of real need or if a package needs to be weighed, from Post Offices, where service is often unbelievably slow.

Public holidays National holidays are: 1 January (New Year or *Nuevo Año*); 6 January (Epiphany and the Feast of the Three Kings, called simply *Los Reyes* - the Kings: what correspond to our Christmas presents for children are mostly given the evening before); 19 March (Feast of St Joseph: Fathers' Day); Good Friday (variable) and Maundy Thursday, which precedes it; Corpus Christi (variable); 25 July (Feast of St James, Spain's patron

144

saint); 15 August (Feast of the Assumption); 1 November (All Saints); 6 December (Constitution Day); 8 December (Immaculate Conception); and 25 December. For the variable Catholic feasts you need to consult a church calendar: the lists of other nations' public holidays given in many pocket diaries aren't too reliable, and very few ordinary British diaries nowadays include the old Christian feast days.

In addition to national holidays towns and whole regions may also shut up shop for locally celebrated feast days. The most important of these are indicated in the main text.

Telephones   Pay phones accept 5, 25, and 50 peseta coins. Instructions for using them (including the minimum charge) are usually pictorially represented. To phone home use a phone box marked *Teléfono Internacional*. Start with a 50 peseta coin, wait for the continuous dialling tone, dial 07, wait for the tone to start again, and dial 44 plus the number you want, omitting the 0 in the code (eg, just 1 for London).

Time   Spanish clock time is normally one hour ahead of British time. Our Summer Time however usually ends later than Spain's, and the difference can become two hours from late September to late October. All timetables quote local time.

Tipping   Though a service charge is included in all bars and restaurants it's usual to leave something extra. It needn't be very large - mostly it's just some of the coins in the change. Railway and other porters have fixed charges, but taxi drivers should be given 10% of the total fare. Cloakrooms mostly have fixed charges for taking care of coats, etc.

Vital addresses   Spanish National Tourist Office (for all tourism queries) - 57/58 St James's Street, London SW1A 1LD (tel. 01-499 0901). Spanish Embassy (for cultural and non-tourism queries) - 24 Belgrave Square, London S.W.1 (tel. 01-235 5555). Spanish Consulate General (for visas, commercial enquiries, authentication of driving licence translations, etc) - 20 Draycott Place, London S.W.3 (tel. 01-581 5921). ABTA (Association of British Travel Agents) - 53 Newman Street, London W.1 (tel. 01-637 2444).

11. Language Guide

BEGINNER'S GUIDE TO SPANISH

If you want to make yourself understood in a language you don't speak don't try to use connected sentences. Concentrate on key words. 'I - tomorrow - Barcelona - what time - train?' is perfectly clear.

The problem is extracting from the answer the words: 'Train - here -9.23 - Barcelona - 10.19'. But this is by far the easiest way of starting on a language. You can go a very long way with a bare vocabulary of around 250 words, and 100 cover most basic needs. Since numbers are a special problem when they're gabbled off, keep rough paper and a biro handy.

You'll soon find yourself fleshing out skeleton statements. To begin with however the only two grammar points you need to know for Spanish are: (1) you add -s or -es to make a plural - **señora** = lady, **señoras** = ladies; **hotel** = hotel, **hoteles** = hotels; and (2) single-word verbs have perfectly clear meanings (no need for 'I', 'you', 'they', etc) - **querría** = I would like, **querríamos** = we would like. You only need **yo querría** (= **I** would like) to emphasise the 'I' or to distinguish **querría** = I would like from **querría** = he/she would like.

Because you can't turn single verb-words round to make questions ('would I like?') written and printed Spanish introduces questions and exclamations with inverted question ¿ and exclamation marks ¡.

Beyond this it may be useful to bear in mind that in Spanish all nouns belong to one of two classes, called 'masculine' and 'feminine' because most names of male creatures belong to the 'masc' class and most female creature names to the 'fem'. Articles (a, an; the) and adjectives (describing words like good, bad, white, heavy, etc) have to be of the same number (sing or plur) and gender (masc or fem) as the nouns they're attached to. eg, **el inglés** = the Englishman, **la inglesa** = the Englishwoman; **los ingleses** = the Englishmen (**or** men and women together), **las inglesas** = the Englishwomen. Don't fuss about this to start with. Everyone will know what you mean if you say **la inglés** or **el inglesas** - or even just **inglesas**.

On the pronunciation front words are spoken exactly as written and vice versa. If a word ends with an -**n**, an -**s**, or a vowel, the last syllable but one is stressed. If it ends with a consonant other than -n or -s the last syllable gets the emphasis. Words not obeying this rule are written with an acute accent (´) to show where the stress falls.

The -ia at the end of some words **can** be treated as a single vowel, and the syllable before it stressed, as in **sangria** (a wine drink). Or the -i- may be stressed, as in **Almeria** (name of town and province). Except in place-names the -i- usually has an accent if it's stressed (**alegría** = happiness). Accents also distinguish meanings of words written alike - **el** = the; **él** = he, **tu** = your, **tú** = you.

Don't bother about detailed pronunciation when you're starting out. Mispronounce everything - but **very** clearly. However, listen specially carefully to the intonation (rise and fall in pitch) and the rhythm of the replies you get. Most language courses and teachers make a ridiculous fuss about detailed pronunciation. Intonation and rhythm are infinitely more important to making yourself understood. Spain, like most countries, has a mass of different dialects with widely varying pronunciations. Spaniards understand each other. Why imagine they won't understand you?

Rough pronunciation guide

a	between **fa**t and **fa**ther
e	gr**a**te
i	sw**ee**t
o	between **o**n and l**o**ne
u	p**oo**dle
y	f**ee**d OR **y**et, according to position

For *b*, *v*, *x* see later.

c	(before *e* or *i*) **th**in (elsewhere) **c**at
ch	**ch**at
d	(starting a syllable or after l- or n-) **d**og: elsewhere between **d**en and **th**en
g	(before *e* or *i*) lo**ch** (elsewhere) e**gg**
gu-	**(before *e* or *i*) e**gg** (otherwise = *g* + *u*)
h	always unpronounced
j	lo**ch**
ll	**y**et
ñ	o**ni**on
q	(used only + *u* followed by *e* or *i*) **c**at
r	**r**ing (clearly trilled)
rr	**r**ing (double length trill)
w	(foreign words only) **w**ash
z	**th**ick

Apart from *b*, *v*, and *x*, other letters as in English.

x starting a word is usually as **s**ing: elsewhere as English. In the Catalan town San Feliú (or Sant Felíu) de Guixols, as English -**sh**-. Catalan is different from Spanish.

147

If you pronounce **b** and **v** as in English everyone will understand.

In pure Castilian however **b** is only sounded like an English b if it is the first sound after taking breath or if it follows **l** or **m**. Otherwise it sounds like a Castilian **v**, which is like an English v sound made without closing the lips, EXCEPT when it is your first sound after taking a breath. Then it resembles an English b. You give up?

It takes months of talking nothing but Spanish to master this. Just bear it in mind when listening to Castilian speakers, or you may mis-hear them. To complicate things further -**nv**- in the middle of a word sounds like -**mb** (eg, in the word **enviar** = to send).

Try however to get your -**d**- sounds accurate. Practise on the word **Valladolid**.

Fundamentals

A, an: one	**un, una: uno, una**
The	**el, la; las, los**
Of the (m sing); some	**del; unos, unas**
No/not; yes, and, but	**no; sí, y, pero**
Almost, perhaps, if	**casi, quizás, si**
There is, there are	**hay**
Now, then, already	**ahora, entonces, ya**
To, from/of, for	**a, de, para**
To the, at the	**(a + el) al**
Gentleman (Mr), Lady (Mrs)	**señor, señora**
(Unmarried lady) Miss	**señorita**
Good, bad	**bueno, malo**
Well, badly	**bien, mal**
Cheap, dear	**barato, caro**

Essential politenesses

Please (for a favour)	**por favor**
Excuse me (apology)	**perdóneme**
— (attracting attention)	**allo** (pseudo-English)
Thanks	**gracias**
— a lot	**gracias muchas**
— **very** much	**gracias muchísimas**
Not at all	**de nada**
Good morning, good day	**buenas días**
Good afternoon, evening	**buenas tardes**
Goodnight	**buenas noches**
Goodbye	**adiós**
— (till next time)	**¡hasta la próxima!**
Hullo (familiar)	**hola**
How are you?	**¿cómo está?**
Very well, thank you	**muy bien, gracias**

I would like	*querría*
We would like	*querríamos*
(On being introduced)	*mucha gusta*
I like (this)	*mi gusta (eso)*
I don't like (this)	*no mi gusta (eso)*
It doesn't matter	*no importa*
Don't bother	*¡no se moleste!*
I'm (we're) in a hurry	*tengo (tenemos) prisa*
I (we) must leave	*hay que marcharme (marcharnos)*
What is (this) called?	*¿cómo se llama (eso)?*

Numerals

Number	*número*
One, two, three, etc	*uno (una), dos, tres, cuatro, cinco, seis, siete, ocho, nueve*
Ten, eleven, etc	*diez, once, trece, catorce, quince, dieciseis, diecisiete, dieciocho, diecinueve*
Twenty, twenty-one, etc	*veinte, veintiuno, veintidos, -tres, etc*
Thirty, thirty-one, etc	*treinta, treinta y uno, treinta y dos . . .*
Forty, fifty, etc	*cuarenta, cincuenta, sesenta, setenta, ochenta, noventa*
Hundred	*cien*
(before other numbers)	*ciento*
101	*ciento uno*
123	*ciento veinte tres*
200, 300, etc	*doscientos, trescientos, etc*
1000, 2000	*mil, dos mil, etc*
1,000,000 (of)	*un millón de . . .*
2,000,000 (of)	*dos millones de . . .*
First, second, etc	*primo, segundo, tercero, cuarto, quinto, sexto, séptimo, octavo, novena, décimo*

People

I, you (friendly)	*yo, tú*
You (formal — sing)	*usted (Vd)*
He, she, (also it)	*él, ella*
We (masc/fem)	*nosotros, -as*
You (friendly — plur)	*vosotros, -as*
You (formal — plur)	*ustedes (Vds)*
They (masc/fem)	*ellos, ellas*
Father, mother, child	*padre, madre, niño*
Son, daughter	*hijo, hija*

149

Brother, sister	*hermano, hermana*
Grandfather, -mother	*abuelo, abuela*
Grandson, -daughter	*nieto, nieta*
Uncle, aunt	*tio, tia*
Cousin	*primo, prima*
Friend (masc/fem)	*amigo, amiga*

This, that, someone, something etc

This, that (thing)	*eso, esto*
Something, someone	*algo, alguien*
Nothing, no one	*nadie, nada*
Always, never	*siempre, nunca*
Sometimes, often	*a veces, a menudo*
Each (one)	*cada uno, - una*
Everyone	*todo el mundo*

(For *this, that* as adjectives — *this book, that house* — use the forms *ese, esa; esos, esas* and *este, esta; estos, estas* according to number and gender — *ese libro* = this book; *esta casa* = that house; *estos libros* = those books.)

Basic questions

How much?/how many?	*¿cuánto? ¿cuántos?*
How much does it cost?	*¿cuánto costa?*
When?/At what time?	*¿cuándo? ¿a qué hora?*
Why?/How?/	*¿por qué? ¿cómo?*
Where? because	*¿dónde? por que*

A little, a lot, etc

A little, a lot	*poco, mucho*
More, less, (an)other	*más, menos, otro*
Big, little	*grande, pequeño*
Enough, too much	*suficiente, demasiado*
Very, (not) exactly	*muy, (no) exactamente*
With, without	*con, sin*

Directions

How far (to) . . . ?	*¿cuántos (kilo)metros a . . . ?*
Here, there	*aquí, allí*
This way, that way	*por aquí, por allí*
Near to, far from	*cerca de, lejos de*
Before, beyond	*delante, mas allá*
Opposite, behind	*en frente de, detrás*
Above, below	*sobre, abajo*
Straight on, for	*derecho, para*
Right, left	*derecha, izquierda*
Main road, motorway	*carratera, autopista*

Crossroads, fork	*cruce, bifurcación*
Street, traffic lights	*calle, semáforo*
(Town) centre	*centro (de la ciudad)*
Church, cathedral	*iglesia, catedral*
Museum, building	*museo, edificio*
Town hall, post office	*ayuntamiento, correos*
Police station, police	*comisaría, policía*

Travelling

Aeroplane, train	*avión, tren*
Slow, fast (trains)	*correo, expreso*
Express, timetable	*rápido, horario*
Station, airport	*estación, aeropuerto*
Bus, car	*autobús, coche*
Motorcycle/scooter, bike	*moto, bicicleta*
(Sailing) boat	*barco (de vela)*
Ferry	*transbordador*
Ticket	*billete*
Single ('just going')	*solo ida*
Return (going & back)	*ida y vuelta*
Departure, arrival	*salida, llegada*
Platform, gate	*perrón, puerto*

Time

Time, (clock) time	*tiempo, hora*
Quickly, slowly	*rapidamente, despacio*
Early, late	*temprano, tarde*
Morning, midday	*mañana, mediodía*
Afternoon, evening	*tarde, tarde*
Yesterday, today	*ayer, hoy*
(Day after) tomorrow	*(pasado) mañana*
Week, month	*semana, mense*
Day, (bank) holiday	*día, día festivo*
What time is it?	*¿qué hora es?*
(It's) one o'clock	*(es) la una*
(It's) five o'clock	*(son) las cinco*
At half past five	*a las cinco y media*
A quarter to six	*las seis menos cuarto*

Days of the week

Monday, Tuesday, etc	*lunes, martes, miércoles, jueves, viernes, sábado, domingo*

Months of the year

Year, January, etc	*año, enero, febrero, marzo,*

| April, May, June, etc. | *abril, mayo, junio, julio, agosto, septiembre, octubre, novembre, diciembre* |

Basic colours

Black, white	*negro, blanco*
Red, green	*rojo, verde*
Yellow, blue	*amarillo, azul*
Brown, grey	*moreno, gris*

Lodgings

Hotel, inn	*hotel, albergue*
Guesthouse, pension	*hostal, pensión*
Double (bed)room	*habitación doble*
Single bdrm, bed	*h. sencilla, cama*
Bath(room)	*(cuarto de) baño*
Reception	*recepción*
Lavatory, shower	*servicios, ducha*
Occupied, free	*ocupado, libre*
Price, bill	*precio, cuenta*

Eating out

Restaurant, menu	*restaurante, carta*
How many are you?	*¿cuántos son?*
Meal, drink	*comida, bebida*
Beer, wine, soup	*cerveza, vina, sopa*
Coffee, tea, set meal	*café, té, menú*
Waiter, waitress	*camerero, camerera*
Breakfast, lunch	*desayuno, almuerzo*
Dinner, sandwich	*cena, bocadillo*
Starters, dessert	*entremesas, postre*
Meat, fish, shellfish	*carne, pez, mariscos*
Beef, pork, lamb	*vaca, cerdo, cordero*
Eggs, cheese, bread	*uevos, queso, pan*
Roast/grill, stew	*asado, cocido*
Omelette, butter	*omeleta, mantequilla*
Vegetables, salad	*legumbres, ensalata*
Potatoes, beans	*patata, judías*
Fruit, peach	*fruta, melocotón*
Orange, apple	*naranja, manzana*
(Half) bottle, glass	*(media) botella, copa*
Mineral water, brandy	*agua mineral, coñac*
Hot, cold	*cálido, frío*
Ice, ice cream	*hielo, helado*
Plate, cup, spoon	*plato, copa, cuchara*
Knife, fork	*cuchillo, tenedor*

152

Shopping

Shop, (big) store	*tienda, almacén*
(Super)market	*(super)mercado*
Foods (in general)	*comestibles*
Butcher's, baker's	*carnicería, panadería*
Pastrycook's	*pastelería*
Clothes, antiques	*ropa, antigüedades*
Open, closed	*abierto, cerrado*
To buy, to sell	*comprar, vender*

Clothes

Dress, skirt	*roba, falda*
Blouse, shirt	*blusa, camisa*
Trousers, jeans	*pantalón, vaquero*
Stockings, tights	*medias, leotardos*
Pants, knickers	*calzoncillos, bragas*
Jacket, suit	*chaqueta, traje*
Overcoat, raincoat	*abrigo, impermeable*
Tie, socks	*corbata, calcetines*
Hat, scarf	*sombrero, pañuelo*
Shoes, boots	*zapatos, botas*
Handkerchief, sunglasses	*pañuelo, gafas de sol*
Laundry, dry cleaning	*lavandería, lavado en seco*

Post office and telephones

Post office, letterbox	*correos, buzón*
Stamp, letter	*sello, carta*
Postcard, packet	*tarjeta, paquete*
Telegram, to register	*telegrama, certificar*
Telephone, to call	*teléfono, llamar*
Long-distance call	*conferencia*
To dial, code	*marcar, indicativo*
Engaged speaking	*comunicando*
No reply	*no contesta*
Reversed-charge call	*cobro revertido*

Toiletries etc

Soap, shaving soap	*jabón, j. de afeitar*
Toothpaste	*pasta de dientes*
Suntan cream (to tan)	*crema bronceadora*
To shave, razor blades	*afeitar, ojas de a.*
Antiseptic cream	*crema antiséptica*
Aspirin, tampons	*aspirina, tampones*
Chemist, insect bite	*farmacía, picadura*

Illness and injury

Hospital, clinic	*hospital, clínico*

Doctor, help	*médico, ayuda*
Ambulance, urgent	*ambulancia, urgente*
Ill, injured	*enfermo, herido*
Ache (head-, stomach-)	*dolor, - de cabeza, - de estómago*
Vomiting, diarrhoea	*vómito, diarrea*
Fever, high temperature	*fiebre*
Broken, sprained	*roto, torcido*
Cut, bruise	*cortadura, contusión*
Blood, skin, bone	*sangre, piel, hueso*

A taste of verbs

Grammarians divide verbs in all languages into 'regular' and 'irregular'. The 'regular' ones are those whose forms can all be worked out from the infinitive. If you know the infinitive **to walk**, for instance, you know that its past tense is **I walked**, etc, and its 'past participle' is **walked** (as in he has **walked**). But if you're a foreigner learning English you have to learn that the past tense of **to sing** is **I sang**, etc, and its past participle **sung** (eg, **I have sung**, etc).

'Regular' Spanish verbs have three types of infinitives and three patterns for their 'present tenses' (those meaning, for instance, **I see, do I see? I am seeing, am I seeing?** — all referring to what's happening NOW). The infinitives end in **-ar**, **-er** and **-ir**. You take these endings away to make the verbs' stems' and add the right endings for **I . . .**, **you . . .** , etc.

	HABLAR	*COMER*	*VIVIR*	
I	*habl-o*	*com-o*	*viv-o*	*hablar =*
you	*habl-as*	*com-es*	*viv-es*	– to talk
he, etc	*habl-a*	*com-e*	*viv-e*	*comer =*
				– to eat
we	*habl-amos*	*com-emos*	*viv-imos*	
you (pl)	*habl-áis*	*com-éis*	*viv-éis*	*vivir =*
they	*habl-an*	*com-en*	*viv-en*	– to live

We're not going to bother about other 'tenses' for the moment. But note that the 'past participles' are **habl-ado, com-ido**, and **viv-ido**. More about them in a moment.

The polite forms of **you** (**usted** and **ustedes**), since they're equivalent to **your Excellency/Excellencies**, use the **he/she; they** verb forms. **Your Excellency goes** not **your Excellency go** (like **you go**). Thus ¿**ha comido?** means **have you eaten?** as well as **has he** (or **she**) **eaten?**.

Unfortunately for learners, the commonest verbs (as in all languages), tend to be 'irregular' simply because they're the most used. This applies to the two Spanish verbs meaning 'to be'. **ser** means **to be** when applied to a permanent or long-lasting characteristic or quality, **estar** means **to be** in the sense of being located somewhat. **soy inglés** = I'm English: **estoy en España** = I'm in Spain.

154

Anyone who has done even a little Latin will realise that **estar** is descended from **stare** = to stand, which makes the meaning-difference easier to understand.

	SER	ESTAR
I	soy	estoy
you	eres	estás
he, etc	es	está
we	somos	estamos
you	sois	estáis
they	son	están

There are also two common verbs for **to have**. **tener** means **to have** in the sense of possessing or holding: **haber** covers other meanings. When you go into a shop you don't say: **¿ha vino?** for **do you have any wine?**. You say: **¿tiene vino?**.

The verb **tener** also has two of what one can call 'regular irregularities'. As with many Spanish verbs, when the first -**e**- is stressed it changes into -**ie**. And since saying **teno** at normal speed is pretty difficult, the word has become **tengo**.

	HABER	TENER
I	he	tengo
you	has	tienes
he, etc	ha	tiene
we	hemos	tenemos
you	habéis	tenéis
they	han	tienen

The other very important 'irregular' verb is **ir** + **to go**. Its present tense has the forms: **voy, vas, va; vamos, váis, van**. Its past participle is **ido**. This seems extremely odd, but isn't really because it's descended from two Latin verbs — **ire** and **vadere**, both meaning **to go**.

haber and **ir** are specially important in the early stages of making yourself understood because you can use them to express future intentions and past actions. Just as in English you say **we're going to see**, so in Spanish you can say **vamos a ver** with virtually the same meaning. And in the same way as **we have bought** can serve in English to cover also the 'past simple' tense (**we bought**), **hemos comprado** will make your meaning equally clear in Spanish.

You need to know too that a stressed -**e**- in a verb stem can also change to -**i**- instead of -**ie**-. **pedir** = to ask for, for instance, has the present tense: **pido, pides, pide, pedimos, pedéis, piden**. Similarly -**o**- can change to -**ue**-, as with **poder** = to be able to, can: **puedo, puedes, puede; podemos, podéis, pueden**.

155

There's a huge lot more that you'll need to know about verbs before you can speak Spanish really well, but for the moment all you'll need is a few basic verbs and an indication of any 'irregularities' in them. The little list that follows gives the infinitive, the past participle, the meaning, and any special 'irregularity'.

First, though, there's just one further tiny point you might consider. In Spanish, you don't **see**, or **invite**, or anything else a person, you see, etc **to** a person. For example, you say: **vamos a ver A papá** = we're going to see daddy; but **vamos a ver el museo** (NOT **vamos a ver AL museo**) = we're going to see the museum.

All these things seems dreadfully complicated and quite impossible to learn when you read them 'cold' off the page. But they soon begin to sound natural if you'll only take your courage in both hands and **use** the language, however bad you may be to start with. But listen as well as talk.

There's a very corny old joke in which someone says: 'Spanish must be very easy. Even tiny children speak it in Spain'. Why not be like a child, and learn to make yourself understood by simply speaking the language —and, of course, listening hard to others speaking it?

So — good luck! Here's the list of verbs.

Like *hablar*
aparcar = to park (a car, etc)
comprar = to buy
llamar = (1) to call, (2) to phone
llegar = to arrive
llevar = to take, to wear
mirar = to look at
necesitar = to need

Like *comer*
beber = to drink
hacer = to make, to do (*hecho* = done; *hago* = I do)
poder = to be able, can
vender = to sell
ver = to see (*visto* = seen: present *veo*, *ves*, etc is regular)

Like *vivir*
decir = to say (*dicho* = said: present tense = *digo*, *dices*, *dice*; *decimos*, *decís*, *dicen*)
elegir = to choose
ir = to go (*ido* = went)
pedir = to ask for (see above)
querir = to want, wish for (present = *quiero*, *quieres*, *quiere*; *querimos*, queréis, *quieren*. But use *querría/querríamos* for politer *I/we would like*)
salir = to leave, depart (*salgo* = I leave)
venir = to come (present: *vengo*, *vienes*, *viene*; *venimos*, *venís*, *vienen*)

156

TOP TRAVEL TITLES FROM SETTLE AND BENDALL

The following books by Trevor Webster all feature in the highly popular series WHERE TO GO IN GREECE published in association with Thomson Holidays.

WHERE TO GO IN GREECE
by Trevor Webster
An up-to-date, easy-to-read, illustrated guide to the islands and mainland centres, containing a wide range of travellers' advice based on the author's recent personal impressions.

£5.99 paper 0907070264 □
3rd reprint 1986
(Revised Edition)

"If only I'd had Trevor Webster's Where To Go in Greece . . . ! Annette Brown *Daily Star*

"an exceptional title for both those seeking culture and the sun". *The Bookseller*

CORFU AND THE IONIAN ISLANDS
by Trevor Webster
Travellers are offered a modern Garden of Eden with Trevor Webster as their personal guide.

£9.99 hard 0907070329 □
£6.99 paper 0907070272 □
featuring 32 pages of full colour: publication
November 1986

RHODES AND THE DODECANESE ISLANDS
by Trevor Webster
The appeal and atmosphere of Rhodes and the nearby islands, including tiny Kassos and Symi with its stunning harbour are brought to life by Trevor Webster

£9.99 hard 0907070353 □
£6.99 paper 0907070310 □
featuring 32 pages of full colour: publication
April 1987

ATHENS, MAINLAND AND THE NORTH AEGEAN ISLANDS
by Trevor Webster

£9.99 hard 0907070337 □
£6.99 paper 090707280 □
Featuring 32 pages of colour
Publication November 1986

Athens within an hour or so of beach resorts is a perfect staging post for visiting the spectacular sites of Peloponnese, Delphi and Cape Sounion and for the ferries to the islands. Trevor Webster takes the reader on a magic tour of the mainland and over twenty islands.

CRETE AND THE CYCLADES ISLANDS
by Trevor Webster
Crete and the Cyclades are islands of great colour, character and contrast. The atmosphere of their stupendous mountains, beaches, harbours, folklore and history is relayed by Trevor Webster.

£9.99 hard 0907070388 □
£6.99 paper 090707396 □
Publication November 1987